Lost In Love

A Journey of Redemption, Forgiveness, and Purpose

By

Taylor Reavis

Lost In Love

©Copyright 2024 Taylor Reavis, Lost In Love

Name of Printer Goes Here

ISBN: 98301870484

Nomad Limits Travel

Nomad Limits Blogs

98301870484

CONTENTS

FOREWORD

I was given the inspiration for this work to release the thoughts that perhaps I couldn't share in person with others. Expressing my thoughts directly from the heart, through my fingertips onto paper, feels more authentic and clear. There is a stunning feeling inside of me, a pursuit of happiness, a passion that drives me to continue challenging myself, overcoming obstacles and sharing inspiration wherever I can through the means of different platforms such as my initial works in my travel blog Nomad Limits, www.Nomadlimits.com, and continue my life with a message of motivation to others dreaming to escape the race of the world by overcoming themselves.

I must admit that I have seen many people come and go in my life, but I have a lifeline that I would like to commemorate and say thanks to my mom and dad for never doubting me when I said I wanted to achieve something elaborate or seemingly impossible. I could have said the most outrageous of things, but my parents supported me, doubtful of my abilities to do them or not. They never limited who I was, and I am thankful for them that I am confident in achieving all I set my heart to. I promise I won't let you down. I am thankful for my two younger brothers Payton and Cayden for sparking in me the enthusiasm to fulfill the best version of myself as possible, to set myself as a role model for them, and constantly strive for greatness through all that I do. In the belief that possibly no one will see my works, I know my brothers will find a way.

Additionally, with the support of my loving grandparents, my grandpa and Mimi, you have opened up a world of two sides for me. Mimi is one with boundless means of invigorating kindness, that enraptures the image of what could only be described as saint-like. Your smile and embrace continue to bring joy into my heart, as I look forward to the days that I can see you through the years as they pass.

To my grandpa, a man of pure heart and unwavering virtue—often tough in the best 'old-school' way—you have shaped the man I am today. Your thoughts are now mine, and through you, I feel that I have become collected and composed as a gentleman; capable of understanding perspectives different from my own solely from the years of disagreements that force me to see outside of my own window of view. You also offered something greater, though. Your warm embrace, your hearty laughs and wide smile or the wry grin when you make a joke, and the effort you put into the family and I, you've marked the character of what it means to live for family. Perhaps you have never cared about legacy, but through you, your grandson will carry on as the man inspired by the greatest grandfather and mentor he has ever known.

To everyone else, Noel, John, Jeff, Adam, Bill, Kelly, Valerie, friends, acquaintances, cousins and those that have seen the metamorphosis over the last few years, I do it all in the hopes that by just one person at a time, I may leave a better mark on the world than when I arrived. I thank you all for your support.

ABOUT THE AUTHOR

Greetings, my name is Taylor Reavis. As I write this book, I find myself reflecting on alternatives to contemporary thoughts, a change in heart, and a leveled mind. With so much occurring in the world, for better or for worse, it seems as though people, through all of the progress we have made through society in the 21st century, are more depressed, more stressed, and more beat down than ever before. We are caught up in the schemes of achieving wealth, fame, validation and attention in any capacity as long as it boosts our ego and brings us closer to the viral sensations we continue to strive for in our lives. I am now coming up to the point in my life where the realizations of the world around me are clearer than ever. I am writing this book as a means of a medium. I want to reach people in order to inspire new thoughts, how to push the limits of their boundaries, and how to be noble individuals in their own right. I may not ever achieve perfection, but to me, continuing to strive for my goals makes life perfect- with good luck, or bad.

I was born in Fort Hood, Texas, during my father's service in the U.S. Army. After his discharge, our family moved back to Louisiana, where most of our relatives lived, except for a few who had settled elsewhere. The few who staggered else included my grandfather who lived in

Daytona Beach, Florida (which will become significant soon enough). My mother worked as a sheriff's office dispatcher while attending cosmetology school during the first few years of my life, while my father was working and attending a state college for a degree in electronic hardware during the turn of the 2000's. In the beginning, the experience was pleasant, as I was the center of attention for the entire family of aunts, uncles, grandparents and distant relatives alike as I was the oldest and only child for a few years until my cousins and brother were soon to be born.

For a period of time, I found myself in a growing in collective family of what seemed to be blissful in the eyes of a young boy. This also was the turning point in many of our lives, as things happen to change quickly, and in the drop of a dime, beautiful days can turn into harrowing nights. Stress began to overtake my quaint family, and my mother and father would have their bouts. Verbal and physical abuse were common, with the slamming of doors and outrageous disagreements. Looking back, the circumstances of these bouts are hazy and unrecognizable, but many a night would I find myself in the familiar situation of being in the dark of my room listening to the berating screams and unwanted contact.

It wasn't until the fateful year of 2005, that a sudden change would change my life completely, for better or for worse, it had yet to be decided. I was only six at the time, but that year, the greatest hurricane to swoop into the Gulf of Mexico caught people from around the state of Louisiana by surprise. The confidence in their lifestyles, the pride and dedication to their homes kept tens of thousands of people certain that they could bear the brunt of Hurricane Katrina, a category 5 hurricane that claimed the lives of 1,836 individuals. Before the hurricane struck, my mom and dad had been in the process of a divorce, and there I was, packed into my mom's 1999 Chrysler Sebring in companionship with our family friend, Karen, my childhood dog, Sadie, and my newly born brother, Payton, who came into this world just a year prior in 2004.

We took only what we could possibly shove into the back of the tight trunk space- any food or extra fuel we could carry, minor belongings, clothes, and the minimalist amount of family mementos that we could possibly bring with us. The person that didn't come with us, however, was my father. There he was, standing behind the Sebring looking onto us, preparing a departure for us to take on the mass of evacuations on I-10 eastbound towards Florida- where my grandfather lives.

He stood behind the car, and watched us load in. I watched him out of the back window fade into the distance, not knowing the fate that would be awaiting him nor I. It was an emotional environment, and when I arrived in Daytona Beach, I was in a state of emotional emergency.

My grandfather, whom I had not remembered meeting before, lived in a 2-bedroom condo, quaint and quiet, with just himself and his dog, Max, a brown dachshund and Jack Russel mix. This was nice for him, and he was comfortable with his pleasant retirement. Prior to moving to Daytona Beach, I was only familiar with my father's side of the family which all resided in Louisiana. Moving to Florida and seeking refuge in my grandfather's small home was a testing ground of patience, yet defiance.

Just a while before we actually left for my grandfather's, he was involved in a devastating motorcycle accident that nearly cost him his leg. He underwent numerous surgeries and fought infection for a period, yet not once did that ever dissuade him from harboring and taking care of his family. The 2-bedroom condo was full to the brim with his daughter, me, and a new baby just over a year old. Life was turned upside down, but he never wavered. He maintained his position as a leader, and a role model, even though I didn't realize how much he would have an effect on my life at the time.

Back then, my emotions broiled inside of me as change took much of an emotional effect on me that I didn't quite recognize at the time. I was quick to talk back, do things my way, get reprimanded, and then do it again.

I made a point to go out of my way to get into trouble because I had a hard time adjusting to my new life.

After much support and a few months, my mom finally found a small apartment close to my grandfather in Port Orange, FL. It allowed us to at least grow our little family, but that didn't take away from the feelings that at the time I couldn't put into words. I ended up divulging those emotions into actions. My single mother was working her way around attempting to make a life work for herself and her sons, while my family back in Louisiana was still recovering as much as they could from the catastrophic events of losing everything. We really did lose everything.

The photos showing what remained after Katrina were devastating. It casted out a lot of my family and tens of thousands of others, forced to live out of FEMA trailers and the bare minimum for years. Everyone attempted to rebuild what they had. I hadn't been able to visit Louisiana until my mom and dad agreed on visitation rights for me and my brother to see our family in Louisiana. It was a slow and arduous process for everyone. With a divorce, loss of my childhood, my dad, and attempting to adapt to a new world in this freshly created life, it was a lot of stress for someone like me who didn't have an outlet to funnel his foreboding energy.

I lashed out many times, and my mind was a flurry of nonsensical carelessness. This occurred while I was also helping my mother out by helping take care of my younger brother, Payton. Even with everything going on, a couple years later, my mom had met my soon-to-be stepdad, Seth. After some further years, my mother was pregnant with my new, youngest brother, Cayden, and that was the start of the real responsibilities. I was tasked with taking care of my brothers and regulating the household while my mom and Seth both worked, and my mom attended college at night.

In those days, I was a mess. In my middle school to high school years, I was quick to argue, in fact I still carry those traits along with me. I was quick to disobey and create rifts in synergy within the household, and at school. Repercussions and consequences didn't faze me, as I was accustomed to them. It had had an effect on my life at home, and at school. I wanted to do things my way, and my commitment to myself led to many issues regarding a progressive growth during my school years.

Because of my differences and feelings of not belonging, I had run-ins with other kids from school. I may have been a mixture of quiet in class and rambunctious depending on the day, but I was quick with my tongue and got myself into some trouble with others that were as itchy for a fight as I was. Through defense of my perceived honor, I quarreled with anyone that gave me the time. I fought my way to solidarity with those that had any issue with me, and I accepted any challenger. I spent many days suspended from school, or in detention, or punished in a variety of ways once my mother received the phone call that yet again, I was involved in some altercation with another student. I just didn't seem to learn.

With me being an older brother, I made mistakes as what a brother should be. I was physical with my brothers, and I took that misplaced energy of anger and hatred of how I felt on Payton, who I felt like I bullied for a majority of his childhood. Thankfully, nowadays, I can say that my relationship with Payton and Cayden is incredible, and they look up to me as proud younger brothers to someone who corrected himself and came to lead as an example. But back then, I had many mistakes that I made that I live with, whether they know it or not.

I remember one day that I think about even now, the musical melody of an ice cream truck phased by our house, and I told Payton that I would buy him ice cream. With cash in my hand, we chased down this ice cream truck with all our might until we caught up to it in our neighborhood. Payton ordered a SpongeBob ice cream stick, and I ordered an ice cream sandwich. I remember that I felt proud to have bought ice cream for him, and it was a beautiful moment for us as we walked back to the house. It was at that moment, however, that Payton had said something to me that I argued with him about. Overwhelmed by misplaced anger, I snatched the ice cream from his hands and threw it to the ground. 'You want your ice cream? Eat it now,' I snapped, the words cutting deeper than I intended.

I'll never forget that moment when I looked him face to face, and the overwhelming emotions of sadness that showed in his soft blue eyes as tears began to swell. The feeling of betrayal within him as he looked at someone whom he trusted became overbearing for me as an older brother in that moment. While he ran inside and wept, as did I, and have I for many times thinking about how I could have been a better role model in those moments, and truly loved the way I should have. Looking back, that moment still frightens me of my past—a reminder of how I failed him as a big brother, letting my anger overshadow my love.

I was an angry person, and I knew nothing about love. At that age of my early teens, I was angry with the world. Nowadays, I am thankful to say I would sacrifice anything for my brothers, and they know it too. There has been significant change, but it was only because of a last resort for my mother through the issues she had to deal with from me.

After running away numerous times, and even attempting suicide at the age of 12, my mother did not have a choice anymore. I was becoming too much of a risk for her to consider letting my life remain on its course as it was a self-destructive path. With the advice of my grandfather, I was urged to be placed in a long-term rehabilitation facility for my outbursts and anger.

Teen suicide remains a critical issue for many young people facing unmanageable stress. Whether due to difficult home lives or a lack of coping strategies, they often feel trapped in circumstances that seem beyond resolution. According to CDC data reported by CNN, between 1999 and 2015, 1,300 children under the age of 13 died by suicide—an average of one every five days[1]. The average kid contemplating or successfully fulfilling that goal are males aged 12. It would have been possible that I could have been a statistic on that chart. So, seeing that I was going through a specifically rough patch, my mom made the decision to let professionals aid in the change.

For 18 months, I was in a strictly controlled environment for rehabilitation during a long-term stay. These white walls confined me into a place of dozens of others that had undergone incredible stressors in their lives that they too, could not overcome themselves. Many of them were from incredibly abusive homes, orphanages, drug-addicted environments, sexual abuse and torment, or other underlying factors that caused them to be placed in the same situation as I was in, but I noticed just how

---

[1] Hanna, J. (2017, August 14). Suicides under age 13: One every 5 days. CNN.

bad others had it, and it truly opened my eyes while within those walls.

Many of them had anger and temperaments that they also could not rope in, and it cost them time to delay their release into the real world. However, it may have been possible that they didn't want to leave, as they were fed three times a day, had the opportunity to participate with kids their age, and overall felt safe even if they were confined to a ward. Though I tossed with my own emotional distress and outbreaks of anger towards my predicament, I continued to grow throughout the months there of taking a role of finally becoming someone that people could look up to, like I should have been for my brothers. I wanted to help those in situations like me, and I became a mediator for peace among those that were really struggling to get a grasp on their reality.

There was an 8-year-old with us named Cody. Cody came from a neglectful household and was prone to outbursts of extreme anger and tantrums. He was only 8 years old, and he has been admitted to a long-term care facility that watched his every move. At first, I thought being here would strip him of his childhood, but I realized that if he didn't get help to effectively change his methods of coping with his issues, his entire life could be in jeopardy.

I stepped up to mediate as a friend to Cody, and possibly even a mentor in helping him see different sides to problems, and as I did that, it also allowed me to see the faults in my thinking and logic. I began to connect with Cody in providing a friend that would participate in his playful games to get his mind away from the reality of where he is, and work with him when he became angry to pursue other methods of coping.

During my tenure there, Cody was about to be discharged just months before I was supposed to leave myself. It was a long period of over a year, and there I was, watching Cody transform. Before he left, he gave me a card in his handwriting with a drawn picture of him and I and he wrote, "I've never had a brother, I've never had anyone but you. Thanks for being my brother, Taylor."

I shed some tears onto the card that day while he gathered his small backpack, and the state came to pick him up. I thought that was the last I'd see of him, but unfortunately, in his head, he loved being at the unit more than being in an orphanage. He thought he could spend more time with me if he came back, but by that time I was counting on days until my discharge, and he lost someone that helped him. I hope wherever he is, he has grown into a successful young man.

Another individual that I had befriended was named Brendan. You see, when in a place like this, there's really a limit to everything you can do, so our minds were the largest outlet of creativity. Brendan, who was my age at the time, introduced me to the patient and particularly creative art of Origami. He had books and sheets of paper that we utilized to make intricate projects. Eventually, we had the bright idea of begging one of the best counselors there, Ms. Kerri, to buy us those long-armed Velcro monkeys from the dollar store so that we could make origami armor and weapons to allow our minds to pursue grand battles with our now freely creative imaginations. Brendan and I connected so well that we couldn't be separated. We grew an interest in Dragon Ball Z, and knights. We crafted massive paper castles and environments for use to utilize our monkey army.

At the end of my duration at the unit, and my discharge, I passed all of my monkeys with the exception of one to Brendan and said my goodbyes. He gave me a long hug and told me, "Thank you for being a friend."

I left him, hopeful for his future. Months after I was discharged, I called the unit and asked to speak to Ms. Kerri. I told her about the massive change in my life it all has been, and how happy I was that through my experiences, did I have a motivation to help others.

I asked Ms. Kerri, "How is Brendan doing?"

She paused for a moment and with a slight choke in her speech said, "Taylor...you really affected Brendan that nobody could have expected. He brings you up every day to talk about memories that the two of you made. And there's one other thing…" She paused again for a moment

XXII | TAYLOR REAVIS

as I sat in anticipation for the next thing she was about to say,

"Brendan changed the name of every monkey he owns to Taylor."

My eyes swelled on knowing that I made friends with someone who considered me such a major turning point in his life, that he attempted to keep the memory of me fresh in his mind by allowing the things that meant the most to him to be named after me. I told Ms. Kerri many thanks for all she did to help me while I was going through a rough patch in my life, and that through understanding the value of helping others, I was able to be the person I should have been by helping my brothers, my family and myself.

I made a vow that I wanted to help others in my life that are going through tough times, and to be someone that people can rely on when they are at their lowest points. I know I am not perfect myself, and I fall back into negative thoughts, but my appreciation to life and those that have helped shape me brought a redemption and a promise that I will do whatever I can to put a smile on someone's face, and also provide the cold hard truth to those who need it. No gimmicks, no lies, no beat around the bush, I would be genuine to myself, and to others.

Of course, being who I am, I still argued with my mom during my years into early adulthood. I have always been too much of an independent person to listen to things that I didn't agree with, but it was always a part of the growth within me that if I truly thought of myself as independent, I needed a change.

That change came after a major argument at the age of 19 with my mom. My grandfather gave me an ultimatum, lighting a fire under my ass to make a decision: move out of my mom's house, or move in with my dad in Louisiana. While I loved my dad, I had a life here in Florida. I had a girlfriend, and I was attending Daytona State College and only had a few semesters left to finish.

My grandfather gave me 2 weeks to move out, but within 3 days, I found a place on Craigslist and was living with 4 other roommates while I finished my education at Daytona State College. I don't think anyone expected such a switch. I perhaps didn't think I could have done it myself either, but there was a sense of virtuous defiance that I wanted to prove that I can make it. Since then, I have graduated from Daytona State, joined the Army National Guard, got accepted to the #1 public university in the United States, the University of Florida, and currently I write this within my last semester of my bachelor's degree.

I have interned at the Department of State within the Bureau of Counterterrorism, traveled to 9 countries around the world with more to come, and renewed my lease on life with a different mindset, new goals, and a pursuit of knowledge and love that I intend to share in this book. I know that life will not always be easy, but within time, I wish to show that challenges are made to be overcome. Even now, I am rewriting this book because my first edition was accidentally deleted and could not be recovered, so I am undergoing this process again because giving up is *never* an *option.*

Thank you for joining me on this journey, and while you read this book, think about what it is in your life that you can approach from the standpoint of understanding, and learning how to be *lost in love.*

LOST IN LOVE

<#>

CHAPTER 1
HOW DID JESUS MEDITATE?

I will begin this book with the inspiration behind the title and show you just why I have been driven to share my experiences of testimony to inspiring others and sharing the reasoning behind it.

There is a story, originating from *Chants of Lifetime*, by Krishna Das. Within it, a powerful story about the connection to my works derives from a simple question, "How did Jesus meditate?"

There are many versions of the story, but to summarize in my own words:

Disciples follow the teachings of Neem Karoli Baba, otherwise known as the Maharaj-ji, a leader in spiritualism and a true devotee to the Hindu god Hanuman. One day, the disciples gather upon the mountains within the temple, ready to start a lesson that will improve their connections to themselves and the teachings of the Maharaj-ji.

The disciples ask the Maharaj-ji, "How can we meditate? We want to know."

The Maharaj-ji looked around at his disciples and in careful words, said, "Meditate as Jesus did."

The others were perplexed, not understanding just how to accomplish this. A test set up for failure, they thought.

One by one, the disciples left the temple and did all they could to imitate the meditations of Jesus. They read through scripture, offered tithes, helped others, gave to charity, prayed, and fasted. None of which seemed to have fulfilled the task at hand. After some time, they couldn't come to grasp how to meditate like Jesus. Defeated, they returned to the temple where the Maharaj-ji was sitting with his eyes closed in his own meditation.

"Teacher," They called out, "we have tried everything, but we have not been able to imitate how Jesus meditated. Please, you must reveal to us how!"

The Maharaj-ji scanned his disciples carefully and, to their surprise, said nothing. He closed his eyes, and the room fell into silence. Minutes passed, and the anticipation felt endless. Finally, tears began streaming down the Maharaj-ji's face as he opened his eyes and gazed upward. Suddenly, tears streamed down from the Maharaj-ji as he slowly opened his eyes looking up to the heavens and said, "He lost himself in love," tears still flowing down his cheeks. "He was one with all beings. He loved everyone, even the people who crucified him. He never died. He is the atman [soul]. He lives in the hearts of all. *He lost himself in love.*"

This is what I have been trying to achieve every single day of my life ever since I heard this parable. The reality is, we have too much anger, too much pent-up emotion, too much hate for others and forgiveness that has not been given. We struggle every day to do right by others, regardless of how they do right for us. Our life is not meant to be personal, but interpersonal. We are divine in the ability to love unconditionally, yet we stray from the reality of what is possible by limiting ourselves with emotions that block being as true as we can to those around us.

Is it not within our ability with no cost to ourselves to be the best version of what we can strive to become? Do we not owe it to our spirit, to our heart, to our mind to let go of the ailments of anger and anxiety. Hatred tears us apart worse than how the other person affects us; regardless how bad they have treated you. Forgiveness is the key to leading a healthy life and growing as an individual capable of losing yourself in love for all people.

Think of those that have wronged you. Does it weigh in your heart and in the back of your mind, going over time and time again about what you did to deserve being treated that way? Do you wish for closure? Do you wish for revenge?

One cannot achieve any of these things without finding closure for ourselves. We are the bearer of our own poisons. It is the essence that eats away at you late at nights and creeps back into precedence when your mind is not distracted on other things. You cannot begin the path to healing without first learning to love yourself and understanding that, as long as you carry the weight of you past, you will be unable to overcome the poison of your present.

First, you must learn to love yourself. Then, you must understand the reasonings behind why, whether your fault or not, some of these things happened. Next, you must learn to forgive those that have hurt and wronged you. Talking about the concept of revenge, forgiveness is the most piercing of revenge that one can offer. Psychologically, those that have committed wrong against you bear the same weight in their mind whether they like to admit it or not. They may play a convincing poker face to others, but it is only them when they look in the mirror that they may see their deeply buried emotions surface to the light in order to inwardly reflect. Your unending love, your conviction to forgiveness, and your growth as a stronger person is the most effective form of getting back at someone who has wronged you. And with that, perhaps the role that you take as a bigger, emotionally advanced person will have an effect on those that hurt you, and they will begin to forgive themselves, and the ones that led them where they are today.

Do not sell yourself short! Resentment is an infestation of a sound heart and mind. The more you struggle with the effect of others on you, the more power they have over you. Do not give into to the obvious corruption lurking in the emotions of negativity. Overcoming your enemies with love weakens them, not you.

It doesn't matter if it's your father, your mother, your friends, family, lovers or whomever. You may feel as if you've been held under water your entire life, and the moment you break free from their grasp and you take the first big breath of air, you run as far as you possible can from the water surrounding you, and the person holding you under. You may feel as though your escape is freedom, but as long as resentment is in your heart, you will still be underwater, just waiting for the next wave of emotions to pull you under its wake.

To overcome this, and remove yourself from the rush of emotions, you must return to the source when you are strong enough. You must take hold of your position, understand your weaknesses, and when ready, face the water as a diver with gear that will allow you to breathe under the stress of those that previously attempted to drown you. You don't have to accept them back into your life, you don't have to allow them to grab hold of you again, but as long as you are capable of forgiving and losing yourself in love, the grasp you hold on to them will be greater than any they've ever had on you.

Love is an unending resource, and it is pulled from within you to perpetuate to others. You have the potential to love unconditionally regardless of circumstance, and show it not only to yourself of which you are deserving, but to others as well. Become lost in love, and shine with it the way you would hope to be loved.

CHAPTER 2
THE PROGRESS DILEMMA

Today, society has overcome many technological barriers, achieving unprecedented interconnectedness. Even so, we seem to find ourselves at a crossroads of all this interconnectedness, to creating awkwardness amongst each other. The ability to connect with real people seems to be becoming a lost art, and it's forcing a divide among those around us that bear the consequences of disagreeing with others' ideologies.

To begin with fixing the progress dilemma, of course, we must identify exactly what can be improved in our society, beginning on a personal level:

- Selfishness is innate but is a feeling that can be controlled.
- Comparisons to others out of jealousy will lead to a detrimental fall in confidence and output.
- Human to human interactions is most important in helping those in need.
- Understanding the perspective of others breaks barriers of ignorance about their beliefs.

These issues define the progress dilemma. We may be growing so quickly at a superior rate of advancement, but we as people are not advancing ourselves. We let machines do our thinking, we let social media control our time, and we let fear get in the way of genuine connections. We cower behind comfortability and revert to social media to escape the world when you'd rather not think about the realities of life around you.

We often compare ourselves to strangers, idolizing their curated popularity. This obsession with social validation—followers, likes, and wealth—creates psychological stress and distances us from authentic self-worth. It is a handicap that tricks you to return in the unhealthiest ways possible. Think about the number of times you open up your social media, and you are riveted by the content of women and men that know that the essence of a weak will brings back consistent clients because of the "sex sells" philosophy or the "get rich quick" scams.

The number of people that have sacrificed their dignity in return for money are the same people that would sacrifice their souls. Do not let this person be you. Dedication to oneself, and not convenience of technology is what harbors positive environments for a return on the best future investment you can take a risk on- yourself.

We compare ourselves to others on a daily basis, and with the influx of media and content that is available, it is too easy to get stuck in a continual loop of self-doubt and lack of confidence. The time you take to involve yourself in useful skills creates a more marketable you. The time you put into growing your mind through philosophy and interconnectedness through genuine human to human compassion is the most important foundations for love.

In Dale Carnegie's book, *How to Win Friends and Influence People*, he writes, "The fastest way to kill something you love, is to compare it to something else." If you love yourself, then why compare to others? Are you not your own unique person? Is there anyone else in the world *exactly* like you? No. Not a single person, no matter how similar or how close will ever be the same as you, nor you to them. We can attempt to compare ourselves in worth, looks, followers, characteristics, personality and everything else we can think of, but it is all a waste of time. You cannot compare what is impossible to change, so only focus on the possible. The great Stoics of our ancient world such as Seneca, Marcus Aurelius and Epictetus for example understood that *what you cannot change, let be, but what you can change, start from within yourself.* External factors of desire and want creates a despair of that which cannot always be obtainable, and that leads to heartbreak and defeat.

A problem that I would like to note on that is growing within the progress dilemma is the overall amount of users finding themselves on a rotation of explicit sites through social media personalities that sell their bodies as a sale tactic for quick cash. I have to ask, is there a limit to your consistent struggles? Do you feel as though you get what you pay for? I would argue that once you set yourself down on the path of personal gratification of believing that you can "pay" for any person you want, that you will find yourself in a rabbit hole of the same content, forcing you into a perpetual cycle of guilt and dissatisfaction. You keep paying for services from people that don't know you and will never know you. Some of you are ok with this and are content with paying this money, but in your heart, can you do better?

I am in no position to judge, or ridicule based on your decision, but I would urge you to contemplate ways to overcome the temptation, by allowing your resources such as the time and money you spend on these services to be placed elsewhere that build your goals and dreams instead of reinforcing others that perpetuate this addictive cycle. I only say this because too many individuals are afraid to admit that they are struggling, and social media keeps the cycle alive.

Outside of the illicit content, we have become so quick to undermine others on a basis of their own opinions, as opposed to a basis of understanding. When you remove ignorance from the equation and utilize the resources you have in your hands to come to a reasonable perspective of others, you hold in your mind the power of observation and truth.

This opens up a door of wisdom to better grow and show love through a variety of ways that could have remained unforeseen if you hadn't taken the time to put yourself in the shoes of the person who is making an argument that may actually align with your conclusion, despite differing perspectives. This works especially in person through that genuine human to human connection.

When you argue with someone who is unwavering in their opinion, the best method to "win" is actually to approach the situation humbly, but with poise. Arguing loses time and ground, and even if you win, you lose. The emotions of someone who has been defeated in an argument can turn into resentment. There is no reason for anyone to carry this emotion within them. The best approach is to find exactly what it is both parties are arguing for. The real answer might be beneath the hundreds of words spewed in a moment's notice, but underlying the overall argument, there is a theme. Listening before you speak and finding that theme is the best way to bring a person onto your side of the playing field without them actually believing they are giving up their stance in theirs at all.

This method comes through careful attentiveness to words and looking between the lines. Ask yourself: What is it both parties want? Is there a common issue that can be addressed that we both agree on? Is there anything that I can get the other party to relate to, and lower their guard to attempt to gain and understand more of their perspective?

These are handy for in-person arguments, as you can react in a way that the other party can hear your tone of voice, can know you genuinely, and make the interaction realistic without the retreat of a phone screen. Once you have mastered the art of reaching others via a one-on-one connection, you can test your ability to undergo the fire of online hostilities which will be exponentially worse, but consistently have I removed myself from the heat of arguments by just being open-minded and caring about all perspectives offered, regardless of how right or wrong I believe they are until I have sufficient evidence and a method to persuade humbly.

One must also admit when they are wrong, which is a major issue with today's society as a whole. We are allowed to admit our mistakes because we are not perfect, and all it takes is one person who is fearless to say, "You're right, and I was wrong." Imagine the number of relationships would have been saved, friendships mended, families bonded if everyone was so freely open to admitting that they aren't perfect, and that mistakes happen! Fixing the progress dilemma comes from the desire of fixing ourselves and being the best version of who we can be for others. That energy will return to you.

Nowadays, everyone wants to reach others via social media, and become popular to share a message or theme, but one does not need to reach the masses of people if you cannot even stand to reach out to those around you in the flesh. Now, I am not saying that technology is an enemy, because we have utilized social media and the connective forms of the internet for good in many ways. There are

7.8 billion people within the world, with an estimated 5.35 billion with ready access to the internet. These numbers are not even computable within our minds, yet we can reach an unprecedented amount of people for our message or movement or ideas.

The greatest influencers and those that amass the most following are those that are interpersonal, and in some way provide a service to others. The problem is, the mind is easily malleable, and too often do we find ourselves at the mercy of pleasurable material that is not healthy for the mind or growth of character. We should stand fast to nobility and values that are often times not growth-based content. We should get out of the social media sphere and connect with those whom we pass every day that could possibly be reached through a perspective of love. If you want to help someone, all you must do is look to the right and left of you while you're out on your daily activities, and in return when in times of your need, people will be there to help you.

We all are going through our own struggles. We all are awaiting something that could possibly make or break us. We are faced with decisions every day that put ailments of stress upon our shoulders that are minds multiply with the unlimited number of potential outcomes. The person walking next to you could have just experienced a death in their family, or bought their first house, or awaiting news that could change their life forever. Our lives are so intricately dynamic, but we are so selfishly focused on our own issues that we fail to formulate the compassion for others when they may be going through something they too have never experienced before. Patience and compassion bring positive growth, even to strangers. Most would prefer not to argue and fight, but some people are mad at the hand they have been dealt, and sometimes it seems they are playing bad hands at every shuffle they get.

We can mitigate the temperaments of people that are in unfamiliar ground by not allowing negative energy that is put out into the world poison your own perspective. You are capable of taking others' energy and redirecting that through your own positivity and of love to create a positive environment to those in times of need. Some people are incapable of sharing their emotions, and they take it out on others as a cry for help because they have never been shown how to ask.

Indiscriminate connections cannot be replicated. True experiences that define memories are some of the most underrated moments in our lives. We do not want the important chunks in our lives to be reliant upon only false connections and followers. Finding avenues of approach to those that are around you every day in genuine conversation and assistance is the best way possible perpetuate love and growth. The energy you put out into the world will come back to you, and it is important to realize just how much of an effect you have on others.

You may even go your whole life without every knowing how much of an effect you have on someone. In fact, it was a while ago that I connected with an old friend named Silvan whom I met years ago. After hanging out on a few occasions, life ended up taking us away to different things and the communication fell off until I called her to catch up quite recently. When we hung out there was a somber moment between us when she opened up to share that she was incredibly worried about her cat, Makayla. Makayla had been Silvan's childhood cat and was currently facing some health issues. Silvan confided with me about how much she cared and loved Makayla, as through everything, this was *her* cat whom she loved and couldn't bear to think about losing her.

When I called her and we started talking, come to find out that after 4 years, Makayla was still alive, but I just so happened to call on the occasion that her health was rapidly declining. She thought it was a strange coincidence for me to have called to catch up because she asked me a question about an event that I had completely forgotten about until she reminded me on that phone call.

"Taylor, do you remember what you told me in the park when I was crying about Makayla?" she asked.

"No, I don't. What did I say?" I replied anxiously.

She paused for a moment, and she reminded me of our conversation. She said, "I was worried about Makayla, and I said, 'I wish she could just live forever!' Do you know what your reply was?"

"I don't." I replied.

Silvan took a breath and answered, "Without skipping a beat, without any hesitation to how absurd of a request it was, you immediately said, 'I think she will live forever.' With a big smile on your face assuring me that everything will be ok."

She followed up with, "That's when I knew you were a good guy, Taylor."

I was honestly taken aback over this phone call. I had clean forgotten about this experience until she brought it up, and I had gone for all of these years never thinking about how much of an impact something so simple could have had on someone, but it does! The ability of the human connection overcomes any vice or method to make someone feel heard and understood. Coming from a viewpoint of love no matter to whom it is brings assurance and warmth to those who desperately need it. The crazy thing is you may never realize any of it.

On top of that, whether in that moment of desperation my words resonated with Silvan, perhaps she truly ended up believing them, because Makayla lived an incredible 4 years longer. Maybe that positive energy brought some light and hope into a very dark spot for someone who otherwise didn't have hope, regardless of how absurd my comment was. Do cats live forever? To me, and to Silvan, especially in that moment, they do.

Since writing this book, Makayla has since passed, but that experience will live on as a moment of true kindness and love that for me, I would have gone my entire life without knowing if I hadn't reached out to reconnect. You may never actually know about the change you bring about to others, but as long as you are a motivated individual that constantly strives to be the best you can for yourself, your legacy will resonate in the memories of others around you for the things you've even forgotten yourself.

Go talk to a stranger today. Find someone on your passing to wherever you're going to ask about their day. People love to talk about themselves so start with them. Find what ails them, find what motivates them. Share happiness and love to those and passing and remind them that the world is a beautiful place and that good people like yourself are out there.

Let go of your temptations for things that take your time and money away from positive growth. Stop comparing yourself to influencers and people that can be superficial in their connections to others solely for views and money. Work on yourself and grow at your own pace, you'll get there! Don't get too focused on the negative, on the divide, on the stress. We all want happiness, we all want love, we all want understanding and for someone to know what we're going through. You are equally as capable of changing someone's life, and you probably already have even if you don't know it. Lose yourself in the love for others, put a little hope into the world, and together, we can solve the progress dilemma.

CHAPTER 3

A SPIRITUAL JOURNEY

I am going to touch, in this chapter, the connection to my life and religion. This book is not by any means about religion, but I couldn't talk about my life if I hadn't written down my thoughts, and my experiences during which I have learned so much if I don't allude to them. The placement of my heart in the overall belief in loving like someone that loved perfectly is an impossible task, but just because the thought of something is impossible, does not mean that I will not attempt to do so, because I am stubborn in my methodology and ways.

I will start out to say that in my belief, I am biased in the ways of Christianity. As you'll see from this book, I have not been afraid to escape the comfort zone of what I knew and believed to earn greater knowledge about the world around me. From my experiences, I have connected well in my faith, though I have stumbled many times in my life, to that for which I live for in the name of Jesus Christ. Many of us all follow within the footsteps of a belief, regardless of whether it is religious or not, and I am here to say that the foundations of religion, whether you believe in Allah, Vishnu, Krishna, Thor, The Buddha, universal energy, rocks, or Jesus Christ, there is an underlying theme in religion that address the morality of man that binds the souls to a heightened state of holiness or enlightenment.

Yes, they all may come across in different methods, and personally for my opinion, I believe there is only one Way, but I will explain how to me, the following of a religion creates not only a well-rounded individual, but it allows for us to carry a basis of understanding in our own lives as we continue through our days as wandering souls in search of happiness.

I have become grounded in a faith that propels me to become a better version of myself not for myself, but for others, and for God. For me, there is a challenge every day that exists, and that is to search for the truth, and to overcome that which drives me into a self-righteous state of gratification. Living for yourself only ends with a continual desire, and to overcome these desires that lead to pain and suffering is to follow a set of guidelines given to us freely within texts so incredibly accessible to us.

Did you know that China, over the last 4 decades is the fastest growing nation in Christianity from 1 million to 100 million believers, and you could be imprisoned or executed for believing it and having possession of the Holy Bible. Imagine the dedication if all of us were so aware of the spirituality of the love of Jesus that we were willing to die or face long-term imprisonment. I mean, that's true dedication, yet we have so many people that neglect the opportunity to utilize their freedoms to research and find for themselves the truth about how amazing it is to be spiritually connected with God.

Ok, yes, now you know I am biased, but it doesn't matter what you believe in. Religion helps us become the best version of ourselves that we can be. If you're a follower of Thor, best believe that there are Norse Pagans that will aspire to be the best warrior they can be, or the Muslim that aspires to live everyday by the word of Allah, and pray, fast, and do deeds in accordance with the Quran (and I'll admit, even better than most Christians in comparison to their own right), or Buddhists or Taoists or Hindus or anything, you are living for a purpose in a higher calling than yourself!

Not believing in anything allows you to become so led astray from being the best individual you can be solely because you are fulfilling your personal needs. Not saying that people that don't believe in religion are inherently bad people, but there is a constant consideration about your relationship with God that allows actions to be considered before being undertaken that make a well-rounded individual capable of overcoming temptations that can easily take others into a place of residual unhappiness.

There are people so mad with religion. Some so mad at believers that talk about their religion when they attempt to share the happiness that they feel within them, but they refuse to want to hear it. They don't want to feel like religion is being forced upon them, or that they shouldn't have to make a decision about believing in something and maintain their freedom. I'll share a story that I heard that really put into a positive perspective about why people who are religious talk about their beliefs and attempt to help those that they love, especially Christians:

You and your friend are hanging out in your house, and everything is going great. There is a vibe, listening to music, talking and overall, the energy is amazing. Suddenly, you realize that you have to take your dog out, and you say to your friend,

'I'll be right back; I have to go take Buster outside.'

You tell your friend to stay in the room and you'll be back in a second. As you're taking your dog out, Buster the dog finishes his business and then, suddenly, as you're making your way back inside you notice a large snake. You grab buster and run inside and close the door behind you.

'Whew!', you exclaim, 'That was a close one!'

Now you go back to your room where your friend is, but they are about to go outside too, saying that they are going to get some fresh air.

'Ok!', you say.

Your friend opens the door and steps outside, not seeing the large snake in the grass lurking. Your friend takes a step and like lightning, the snake strikes. In a panic they run inside and close the door, yelling to you, 'There's a snake outside! It bit me!'

Your response is, 'Oh yeah, I know.'

'You know!? Why didn't you tell me?', They yell out in anger and frustration.

You simply respond, 'I didn't want to take away your freedom of going outside. I didn't want to impede upon your will of going outside because you should be capable of finding out yourself without interference.'

Isn't that silly? If you truly loved your friend, and if you wanted the absolute best for those you care about, and especially for strangers, shouldn't you, as a spiritual being, a careful man or woman in this world, attempt to do the best at all times to prevent others from being bit? It is from a position of love that people share their most highly valued belief with you. If your decision is to still walk outside after you know the dangers, then that is your decision. Until then, if it were me, I will warn and hope to be warned of the dangers so that I can expect what possibly could go wrong.

It wasn't until recently that my faith became grounded in a long-term devotion to my belief in Christ. When I was in basic training for the Army at Fort Jackson, South Carolina, the only text we really could read was military related literature or religious texts. My ex-girlfriend, Rosana, at the time bought me a beautiful King James Bible that I read every night after I documented in my journal my daily experiences in basic training.

Apart from the first few weeks, the guys started doing a weekly bible study with an amazing guy in our platoon by the name of Deion Cutter. Cutter was an ordained minister back home, and one night after bible study, I walked up to Cutter and asked him if he could pray for me.

Cutter said he would, and he placed his hand upon my head and started praying. The experience was something I was not expecting, and as the words spoke out of Cutter's lips, the surge of energy was coursing through my body. He called upon God to answer my prayers and spoke about my relationship with my girlfriend at the time, and if I decided to stay with her, that my future will bring a beautiful family and I a good father. He spoke about a place in my life for God and utilizing my skills of connection and communication to bring people together close with God as he put it, 'a shepherd of the people.' And then, he spoke about something I had never shared with anyone, and something that still weighs on me today, but now I have more faith in than anything.

Cutter paused for a moment, and then through shut eyes he whispered, "And God is telling me that the prayers about your grandfather will be answered."

In that moment, I can't explain it completely, a jolt of electricity surged my body from the top of my head where Cutter's hand was placed that exploded throughout my body and left out of my legs. I burst into weeping tears, water streamed from my face and my legs shook. I lost control of my stature and fell to the ground, looking up to heaven and thanking God for the answers I have been looking for.

You see, for years, I have pleaded with God to let my grandfather come to Him. Before that moment with Cutter, I was a lukewarm Christian that prayed when I needed something, or when times get rough. However, I always wanted my grandfather to believe in Christ, because I wanted to be with him for eternity. He has been a staple of my life and a forger of my character. My grandfather has brought out the best of the man I could be, because he is the individual that captures the essence of the man that I can't let die in spirit, as to which I live vicariously through his methods and learn to imitate the greatest mortal man I know.

With that being said, my revelation of Christ has brought me to understanding the true nature of his power from that which I haven't spoken a word of to anyone. Silently in my prayers did I call out to Jesus, until Cutter called them out loud from the word of God. That was the single most incredible experience through my tenure in basic training, and I owe it to Cutter for being the mediator in that change.

Talking to my grandfather about Jesus seems to single-handedly be the hardest thing that I can do, and I have been uncertain of how to bring up the topic. I know that through his struggles, and perhaps even the loss of his brother, that having a relationship with God is difficult. I am afraid to bring it up. I have been a coward to talk about God with him, because I know how quick he is to rebuke that which he doubts. I feel as though I have never been prepared to bring up how I felt to him, but recently more than ever, as my faith has grown, so has my confidence.

I am preparing to raise the question up to him and ask him the truth about his beliefs. Could you imagine that talking with the person you love most would be the hardest person ever to ask questions about God to? I'm not afraid to say that I have been delaying that confrontation, but it is the last thing I'd ever want it to be. I don't want a confrontation; I want a genuine conversation from the heart. Just like all things now, I want to come from a viewpoint of understanding. I have prayed to God for wisdom and knowledge, and I feel that I have been granted these wishes through the constant ability to learn and grow as a person growing in my walk with spirituality.

Along with the desire to continually grow in wisdom and knowledge, I also am a contender for minimizing the ignorance of others by filling my heart with the love for others whom I don't understand. I am still working on curving the jagged edges of my judgment for all differences in my life, but it is a lifelong commitment, as I have absolutely no right to judge others.

That being said, on a pursuit of knowledge, over the summer of 2023, I escaped on a 2-month backpacking hiatus to Thailand, where I undertook an incredible adventure that shaped my mind and opened up my understandings of those around me. I have never been afraid to learn, and to make myself more aware of the things I never knew, I challenged myself in the most unfamiliar way I ever imagined.

I was ordained as a Buddhist monk at Wat Mai Ket Ngam, a temple in Chonburi, Thailand. This was a transformative journey, as I immersed myself in a foreign culture and lived among monks who spoke no English. To them, ordaining a foreigner—or Farang—was likely as unfamiliar as it was to me. For me, however, I accepted the challenge and was prepared to begin my new perspective of meditation and removal of materialistic desires. I wanted to live simply and grow my relationship in God by understanding religions to actually set myself apart from only what I have been taught.

The entire journey for further context can be found on my travel blog, Nomad Limits. It covers the emotions and experience from the moment I left the US, up until the point when I had returned and shows just how incredible it is to live with openness and love.

I was only ordained for 7 days, as the ordination as a Buddhist monk was in the latter half of my stay in Thailand, and I was running out of time to accomplish this goal. I was laden in white and brought before essentially the head monk of the temple where I signed my name, they officiated me as a Buddhist monk legally on paper, and then gave me the name of "Ophaso." In Sanskrit, the name means "The Enlightened One" or "Seeker of Knowledge." After the official title was given, they led me outside to where they shaved my head, which is to represent the detachment of vanity of our personal body. After my head and eyebrows were shaven, they removed my nicely grown mustache. I was sad to see it go, but all anxiety of going through with the ordination left me after I had nothing left to lose. I went through the ceremony with the support of Honey and the people that I had never met to come out and support me. I really didn't know any of them, they were all family members of an auntie that works below Honey's apartment building.

Honey is a Thai girl that supported me every step of the way through the adventures. We grew so incredibly close, and she motivated me to continue being the best individual I could in the search of challenge and overcoming adversity. She made it possible for me to become a monk and it was all by pure coincidence. Without her, however, it would have never happened. She was conversing with the Auntie that worked below her about my interest in becoming a monk, and through that conversation, Auntie shared that her brother is connected with a local temple and can talk to them about undergoing the ceremony to ordain a Farang. Auntie brought almost her entire family out to come provide an incredible amount of support and compassion for some Farang looking to do the unthinkable.

I met them as strangers, but their unwavering support and love for me as a Farang undergoing this arduous process brought us together as the closest bond one could only relate to as family.

They supported me and showed me so much admiration. I was emotional and so very appreciative of everything they had done for me to provide a loving and positive attitude for this rapid change from what I was used to. I realized then that if everyone could help each other in such a tremendously loving way, there would be so much to offer each other in return for the exchange of indiscriminate love.

I was brought towards fourteen monks with my shaven head, and after going through the introductory chants, was led to the side of the temple and piece by piece, my white clothing was removed, and I was donned in the fiery orange robes of a Buddhist monk. Orange signifies the rebirth of an enlightened person, undergoing spiritual growth through fire, since fire destroys, but it also creates opportunity for new life. I was courted back to the center of the temple and spoke the mantras in Sanskrit for my ordination and took my vows as a Buddhist monk, brought together by the fourteen who gathered around me and chanted. I chanted in Sanskrit the vows of chastity, poverty, immaterialism, and the removal of vanity. In that moment, I felt the energy of this ancient language fulfill a spiritual resonance within me. It lingered in the air as they chanted that opened my eyes to how powerful the energy we fail to recognize is in the universe.

I bowed three times to the head monk, the Abbort, and then was introduced to my mentor, Prat' Mot. (Prat' is the Thai word for 'monk'. Another form of officially addressing a monk is *loom-pii*, which is Thai for 'Heavenly Reverend.")

After meeting Prat' Mot, we said goodbye to my newly fashioned Thai family as they bid me best of luck on the challenge of monkhood. I said goodbye to Honey from a distance, since monks are incapable of having *any* physical contact with the opposite sex. Whole-heartedly, I said my thanks and bid her farewell and asked her to visit me when she could. After she departed, Prat' Mot showed me my living arrangement.

I was staying in the back of the temple with Prat' Mot, who would guide me through my stay at the temple. With me, I had only in my possession the gifts provided to me after the ceremony. This included a tin food storage container, a teapot and drinking cups, a Talipot fan (used to remove distractions of listeners from the monk to focus on the words spoken), my spare orange robes, a small pillow, a thin bamboo rollout mat to prevent my robes from becoming dirty on the ground while I slept, a thin orange blanket and the most important piece of all, my alms bowl, or *begging bowl*. (We'll get to the significance of this.)

I rolled out my mat, set up my pillow and positioned my items as symmetrically as I could for ease of access through my limited possessions. Monks cannot eat after 12pm, and typically it is only one meal a day. I was lucky enough that before the ceremony, one of Honey's favorite places to eat that is conveniently placed under her apartment served minced beef and basil or *Pad Kra Pao*. I was afraid of not knowing the next time I would eat that morning, so I shoved the entire bowl in my mouth and downed an entire cup of Thai tea in a single go.

I went the entire day after the ceremony with just that, and plenty of water to drink. The adjustment was going to be completely different; I knew it, but I was ready for the upcoming incredible days.

After becoming familiar with the wat and meeting some monks around the area, I was preparing for my first night. I was unsure what to expect for the sleeping situation, but after evening prayer with Prat' Mot, we got to know each other better through Google Translate conversations. Soon enough, 9pm had creeped up upon us, and the morning called for an early rise, so I needed some rest. I would say overall, my first day as a monk concluded relatively well, even as I rubbed my head constantly throughout, still coming to terms with the aftershock that I really did shave my head to undergo this crazy idea I had.

I didn't know how real it was going to get until I finally managed to lay down to get some much-needed rest. The floor that I laid upon was a hard wood floor. The small bungalow had no air conditioning, but luckily Prat' Mot did have a few fans that he compassionately placed all around me to keep my body regulated through the Thai night heat.

The only padding that I had between this hardwood floor and myself was that rollout mat, thin and flimsy in order to keep my robes presentable. I, at least, was not sleeping directly on the ground, and I also had a small pillow to support my head so it could have been worse. The issue was, this mat did not have padding, and every rotation or turn of my body caused a grinding of my bones into the wood that dug into my hips, spine and shoulders. Typically, I prefer to sleep on my side, but during the nights there in the wat (Thai temple), I slept stiff like a soldier at the position of attention.

That first night, was the roughest I had gone through. The Buddha says, "All suffering derives from inherent desire and ignorance." And in that moment, my inherent desire was to be on a bed. I have never experienced what it was like to be without some form of comfort that I could look forward to. Even in the Army, when I slept in dirt holes, I felt comfortable because I was able to take precautionary measures for comfortability over the course of the nights in the dirt. Here, however, I had to endure the pressure upon my body throughout the long night.

I was drifting in and out of sleep, my body wincing from the pain that captures every movement into discomfort. It was in these moments as I attempted to set my mind into an incapacitated state, that my mind drifted into images of the unbelievable. There, within my discomfort had I seen visions of others that have never perceived comfort, and lived like the way I was sleeping every day of their lives. I saw those that have never felt the comfort of a padded bed, or the security of 4 walls and a roof. I saw those prone to the unrelenting power of nature, exposed to rain and wind, blistering winters and scorching heat. I saw homeless people on the streets of major cities, sleeping on park benches and bus stations, cold concrete and grimy ground. I saw kids that have never experienced comfort even within their own homes, sleeping in dirt and arising to no ease of their pains.

Here I was, a monk in an attempt to learn about others, and within my first night of suffering, the physicality became vicariously personified for those whom I have never met. My heart was opened by the revelation of suffering, and it connected my methods to even how the Buddha told his followers how to meditate and live for enlightenment.

The Buddha wanted us to remove that which comforts us, as it is the method to understanding the true pain of others. Ignorance is a vice for suffering, because only through knowledge and understanding do we grow from pain that others feel inside of them, and can we better serve ourselves and others.

There was a point in the constant drift in and out of sleep that eventually the pain stopped, and I saw the flashes of these images while internally connecting with each person I had seen. It was something incredible, but I didn't know how to feel about the experience, When I woke up early in the morning, I met my suffering with a pleasurable welcoming, as I had learned about the pain of others, and that opened my eyes to so much more than my own world, and that my pain is nothing compared to others that have never had the luxuries that I should be everyday grateful for.

I rolled out of bed early in the morning, and Prat' Mot had already been up to sweep the temple since he likes to get up at 3am. I followed suit about an hour later in preparation for the Bintabaht. The Bintabaht is a sacred tradition for Buddhists. Early in the morning as the sun rises, the monks go out into town wearing robes also called "Bintabaht." During this morning routine, the monks, donned only in their robes and begging bowl set out on their city, town, or village in order to collect donations, or *alms* from the local people in order to satisfy their daily needs.

We would walk in groups of two to three, sometimes more, and we would meet people that would intercept us upon the street to give donations of food, money, medicine, or anything else the monks may need in exchange for prayers. These people that come out to give the donations to the monks are the lifeline of the monks, as we have only what is given to us, and anything left over is donated to those in need.

Most of those looking for prayers that donate food or money are doing so on behalf of their family, or to have positive energy come into their life, or to honor those that have passed on. The mantras of the monks in the prayers towards those that bow their heads to us, kneel before us, and shed tears before us was an incredible experience of how powerful it felt to offer someone comfort in their hardest times. While the mantras were spoken, secretly I prayed to Jesus about the ailments of these people.

I did not overstep my place, however. I was not ordained as a Buddhist monk to evangelize Thailand in the name of Christianity. I became a monk to understand the reality of the Buddhist beliefs and how important that belief was to the Thai people by placing myself in that role. My reality focused on the amazing connection of those that took their beliefs so incredibly serious, and challenging my commitment to it, regardless of the differences. A lot of times, I realized the shame from the feeling that I have seen Christians in the United States who claim their faith but fail to reach the levels of dedication as others who entirely have less than we do in the first world countries for their own religion.

During the Bintabahts, I did this often. I would repeat the mantras, but to myself, would also pray for them. At first, I really struggled with the idea of idolatry or blasphemy when I would bow my head to the statues of the Buddha, or repeating mantras in Sanskrit. In my heart, however, I never wavered my faith to God. To me, I felt in my heart that through my constant communication to God, that I was not turning my back on Him.

During a night of discomfort, I prayed to God that He would send me a rainstorm with thunder and lightning, and I told him that He knows I am comforted by the patter of rain against a roof and slow rumble against the windows when I sleep. I knew I would sleep if he just sent me a rainstorm.

There was no rain to come that night. However, the next night, I went outside to the shower inside of a small disconnected shower and bathroom space apart from the house I lived in. While I took away my robes and began to wash myself, I heard the rapid trickle of water outside of the pattern of falling water from the shower. Quickly, I adorned my robes and opened the opaque sliding door to the outside world, and there before me was the showers of a great thunderstorm. I stood before it and held my breath in disbelief, oh my little faith.

I stepped out into the dark and torrential weather, protected by the shallow overhang from the roof of the house above me. I looked my eyes up to the sky and exclaimed in excitement, "God! Thank you! Show me some lightning!"

While I looked and waited, my breath was heavy and impatient. I felt a surge of uncertainty within me. I called out, "God! Show me some lightning!"

My eyes still looked above with hope and desire that I would receive my answer. I felt a sense of surrender overcome me. I lowered my head and placed my knees upon the wet concrete below. I lowered my head to the earth and felt the rain pelt against the back of my bald head. I called out to God,

"Dear Lord, thank you for bringing me here. Thank you for giving the opportunity to learn about others, and to bring myself closer to other cultures and the people of this world. Thank you for allowing me to not turn my back on you, and to give you my full love donned in these robes without feeling that I am turning away. You have given me the ability to grow as a person and to live truly for love as you intended. I pray you continue to guide me. Amen."

I opened my eyes and raised my head up to the skies, now soaked by rain in my robes and called out,

"God, show me some lightning!"

Before me, unlike anything I have ever seen, on the dot of calling out to God, a magnificent streak of the brightest bolt of lightning, expanding upon the skies, illuminating the blackness surrounding me with the weight of falling water, was the most illustrious streaks I have ever peered upon with my own eyes. The streaks started from the right of the sky, and creeped its way to the left and in seconds, exploded into an array of webs that seemed to pull the entire night sky back into place. The boom of the thunder that came from this lightning rattled the house and my bones.

I slept like a baby that night.

The entire journey was knowledgeable and a spiritual expedition of growth in love and understanding. I came out of the experience ordained as a Buddhist monk with an even closer relationship to God because of that mutual understanding I had about what I was doing. I know that some Christians themselves could hear this and place doubt within the strategy, but once they hear the rationale about removing ignorance in my life by actually living first-hand that which is radically different, they cannot deny my connection to God once the conversation begins.

A Christian asked me, "You can understand something, but not love it. Why would you want to participate in something you shouldn't love as a Christian?"

My rebuttal is, "Who walked with us that ate with the sinners, the vile men and women, those furthest from the light?" Paul in the Bible says about Jesus, "Let *nothing* be done through selfish ambition or conceit, but in lowliness of mind let each esteem others better than himself. Let each of you look out not only for his own interests, but also for the interests of others. Let this mind be in you which was also in Christ Jesus." Philippians 2: 3-5. Jesus is the mediator between love and truly loves all people, regardless of how much God hates sin. The grace of Jesus is the saving of souls through indiscriminate love!

So, with that being said, I would participate in that which most misrepresent and fail to understand, because as a Christian, I look to imitate Jesus as best as I can. This method is to stand fast to the truth, and the light, but learn and as I grow, allowing others to do so as well.

My methods of coming to understand the perspective of religion and spirituality also are rooted in the philosophy of Stoicism contrastingly. The greatest minds that lived relative to our age has created the connections of living life within the bounds of ones' own means. Through the comparison of religion and philosophy, those that follow either, are compelled in virtue to create goodness that derives from a virtuous life.

Separating the good and bad in life is under the philosophy of labeling what could be considered good and bad. This might not always be readily apparent, but the most common methodology to accomplish this is comparing good and bad under virtue, and vices; this theme is mentioned in "Meditations" by Marcus Aurelius.

The reason why religion and philosophy are important is that it continues to provide an avenue of approach for realizing the things in life that might have a negative influence or impact, versus a positive one. The idea is that goodness in life is brought from the pursuit of virtue. By constantly challenging our physical body and mind to remove in our lives the things that drive desire, want, or longing, we can grow in our virtues and interpreted goodness. So, just as we might want to pursue goodness in virtue, the same acknowledgement should be made for finding the bad in life that we can make a conscious decision to change, called vices. Vices are those things in your life that constantly drive you away from being the best individual you can be, and they are just as subjective as virtues are because everyone approaches ideas of right and wrong differently, but that is the reason why utilizing a baseline of religion is so important in delegating the right mentality.

Not all things that make you feel happy and pleasurable are good for you, and not all things that make you feel terrible are inherently bad things. The purest metals are forged from fire, and as long as you have not undergone the flames of testing yourself, the impurities will continue to exist within you. This is the belief in how pursuing virtue and removing vices comes from understanding what kind of impurities within you make you less than your own best self.

Of course, this is open to interpretation, as it is only a method improvement based on the ancient philosophies of the great Stoics before us, yet they are as truthful now as they were when they were conceived those many years ago.

Think of the things that you struggle with, or maybe even the things that you could change that would bring about a positive impact on your life. It doesn't have to be some complete life-altering event, but just something that builds character. If you're a smoker or a consumer of alcohol, and also want to be considerate of your health, will limiting the amount of the intoxicants that you enjoy eventually bring about a positive impact to your life? If you are lazy and procrastinate your work or school, will taking the proper steps to accomplishing your responsibilities make you feel just a bit more appreciative of the effort you put into it? Usually, the answer will be yes, and those that disagree may be fighting the reality that the things they are most afraid of giving up will make the most difference once they do so.

Change is not easy, but there are easy ways to begin initiating change that will prepare you for the eventual forging by fire to let go of the vices that affect you as an individual. The book, "Make Your Bed" by Admiral William McRaven talks about how the challenges in your life are amounted by how many small things you let go unchecked. His analogy is that big challenges are overcome by accomplishing the small tasks. Making your bed in the morning the first accomplishment a person can make besides having the blessing and opportunity to wake up and open your eyes.

Once you get up, making your bed allows you to take pride in the first small task that can lead to a feeling appreciation and respect for your efforts. The act of making your bed is a great example of overcoming the first of many challenges in the day, but a continual victory over and over again of these small things allows your mind to manifest the idea of overcoming the large and more challenging obstacles that you struggle with.

The ideas of religion, spiritualism and philosophy is to aid in the minor things, that eventually will be a guide in how to tackle the most difficult of problems you may find yourself in. These stressors can come from addiction, association of people, abuse, depression, loss of loved ones, and so much more that people every day continue to get discouraged from in improving their personal lives and mentality.

Your vices may outweigh your virtues, but they are not definitive, and only you can come to terms with what you believe is virtuous and creative, or of vice and destructive. You know in your heart what it is that you can change about yourself, as we all do. Know, however, that you are not alone, and that you *can* put your struggles onto the shoulders of God and get carried through your pains. Just be aware, that if you have turned away from God for so long in your life, He will want to know exactly where you stand in your heart when you come knocking on His door.

It may not be the first knock, or the second or the third that He may open up His door for you, but if He does and you become scared of the truths and run away, the goodness of God's porch light will be turned on for you when you are ready to return home. It is hard to admit our struggles, but if you truly are done fighting alone, then it takes only the faith of a mustard seed to move mountains. Trust in God, trust in yourself, and trust in the challenge, as they are forging you to be the best you can be. Don't give in to the perceived failures, because it is life's best learning tool. The reality is, the only time you've really failed, is when you, in your heart, have accepted defeat and refuse to be the best warrior you are.

This book is about encompassing love around you, but most neglect to look inward to love themselves, or sometimes the opposite and love themselves too much. Whatever the case is, the motivation is for you to become better by loving yourself just enough, but for others to give completely. Be a guide of happiness, truth and love and provide to those around you the unexpected feelings of appreciation and respect. Ultimately, they would lay themselves on the line for you, knowing you would do it for them. This does not mean to undermine your self-respect, but to be selfless in your execution of actions.

Be the most of what you can, and don't neglect what you can become in spirit.

CHAPTER 4

ACCEPTING LOSS

At the time of writing this book, I had lost my grandmother- my dad's mother. I was working within the motor pool of my Army unit in the National Guard when my father called, informing me that my grandmother has passed abruptly.

The call was saddening, and the experience was surreal. I hadn't lost too many family members within my lifetime just yet, and the memories of my grandmother of who I used to know rushed back in the loving lady that took me as the apple of her own eye. 'Mawmaw' as I called her changed drastically after Hurricane Katrina, in which according to press reports, an estimated $190 billion dollars in damages adjusted for inflation and 1,392 deaths rocked the southern states of the Gulf of Mexico in 2005 (Schleifstein, 2023). The physical death of many enumerates to the second highest death-toll by any hurricane, following now behind Hurricane Maria in 2017 in Puerto Rico. The emotional death of those that survived, however, caused the lifelong suffering of emotional trauma that some had never recovered from.

I think it is fair to say a majority of my family, including myself, all suffered the consequences of what could be described as PTSD. I never knew it at the time of my young age after the occurrence, but I do believe that in conjunction with the divorce of my parents and the hurricane, I lived through a hell of my very own. My parents, aunts and uncles, grandparents, and those that stayed in Louisiana and even those that left all faced repercussions of the reality-shattering catastrophe that struck that August in 2005. Tens of thousands of people huddled within the New Orleans Super-dome, and awaiting FEMA trailers were possessed with the high-intensity emotions of loss and anger projected by people with nothing else to lose. Family, friends, entire homes, vehicles, life-long memories, dreams, and livelihoods were swept away as easily as it was to blow out a candle. To live with this, among those that relied on the necessities of safety with these things, caused rampant degradation of the people, and the morale within Louisiana and Mississippi.

The changes of those around me began to take hold, and some never recovered. Mawmaw was one of those people. Her career as a tax and accounting manager for many clients within the St. Tammany Parrish area made her well off before the hurricane, but following the storm, the eventual plunge into the strangulation of fear tortured her mind. She became the shell of her former self, and for years, little to no contact was made with her from my mother's side of the family as we had moved to Florida. My father's side of the family and himself stayed behind in Louisiana, and the rippling effects of separation and monetary troubles began for many.

Turning to illicit drugs, losing her homes, threatening her own children, and even making an attempt to kidnap me at one point all formed a barrier of myself from her through my mother's protectiveness. This was not the grandmother I knew, and it wasn't until later that I understood just how traumatic the experience was for those that stayed behind. Living in FEMA trailers, fighting for a new way of life, and attempting to overcome adversity day after day, especially in her retiree age did not aid in any capacity the tolls it inflicted upon her mind. It wasn't until years later that a 'reconnection' happened, as I asked my father to visit her with my brother, who only saw her when he was a baby and hardly remembered who she was.

As I walked into the door of a hidden apartment complex off of the main road in Slidell, LA, there she was. A glossy eyed woman with the loss of a will to fight. There are no metaphors to describe the emptiness and self-shame that looked back at me as I greeted her for the first time in years. The woman that stood before me was not Mawmaw, but a broken woman that had allowed her life by accords of personal actions and that of circumstance to become intolerable to herself. For the circumstance of attempting to make amends through the forgotten years of suppressive communication and avoidance, I left for her a picture booklet I made at a local photo booth filled with pictures of my brother and me. I gave it to her and placed it on her coffee table, unsure of what to say, or how to feel. The only thing I could recall was the overwhelming sadness that filled the room and made the environment heavy as though I was breathing in a thick, hot soup that permeated my chest. This feeling of pity for what used to be my grandmother- a loving and careful woman with respect within her community and a loving family now living from a couch in a one-bedroom apartment and eating packaged hot dogs and whatever my aunt would make her for nutrition. I couldn't explain how I felt, but I knew that the loss of my grandmother had already occurred.

When I got the phone call years later that Mawmaw had died, I still took it incredibly hard. I thought about the possibilities of what could have been during the time leading up to the decades following the hurricane, and why in cases such as this some people suffer long enough to only hope that death arrives to take them from their pain. I needed to remove myself from the area and spoke to the Army chaplain about the loss. My unit was incredibly helpful in bringing up my spirits and allowing me to stay and work to get my head out of the thoughts from my childhood.

I was sad more so for the fact that I truly loved Mawmaw, as she is remembered by me to be the strong woman that loved to babysit me and my cousins, always wanted to host the family and bring others together in a caring way. I didn't want to remember her for who she'd become, and I turned that love from my forgiveness of what had happened to her, and the actions she had decided to take into account for the belief that deep down, I knew that she was always a fine woman with a heart for her family.

Some people face loss of those closest to them in peculiar ways, and everyone grieves differently. I prayed to God constantly about the lives that I have experienced in loss within my youth, and I continue to hope for nothing but the greatest of opportunities to continue to show that as a son, grandson, nephew, brother, and friend, I give my utmost appreciation to those around me. As I continue throughout my days, I hear about the deaths of friends from high school, college, the military, and acquaintances from passings years ago. I think about how quickly life can turn into the afterlife, and it troubles me to believe that as quickly as life can speed by in age, it can be ended just as abruptly through occurrences of Life's greatest misfortunes. My solace is that my love for God is the proponent in which I want to share that fear of loss to those I love, even though the conversations are tough, or perhaps overly critical.

Loss is meant to be accepted, though difficult and challenging. Death is the guarantee of life, more so than life itself. Out of the billions of possibilities that you could have never been born, or never had the opportunities to walk on Earth and to read this book, here you are. You have the ability to share yourself in the most expressive of ways and to give others a chance to do the same. While you breathe the air around you, your chance of loving has not been snuffed. There is never a guarantee for tomorrow, and it is imperative to take each day with the hope that you are living to circulate the potential of love you have to give.

Unfortunately, eventually you will die, and you must be prepared in the ways of leaving with grace regardless of where you are. Think of how you want to be remembered. What is the legacy you are intending to leave upon those that have known your name, and what perception will allow the energy that you put out into the world bring back to you in remembrance? The death of great people within your life will haunt you until the day yourself passes. I cannot emphasize enough the importance to take the moments to say your appreciation to those that in your heart, deep down and no matter how hard it is, to say, "I love you."

When my great-grandfather passed away at a wonderfully abundant age of 98, I had seen him through occasional visits from my grandfather (whom I've called Gramps or Grampa since I was little) to check-up and help with yard work. That old man, my great-grandfather, outlived 4 wives, and that is an incredible bit of history that still baffles me. I remember as he was descending into his need for round-the-clock care, and the whittling of his body down to the bareness of his bones as he began his transition into the next step of life, my feeble great-grandfather was cared for by Gramps and my grand-aunt.

When he passed, I remember I spoke some words at his funeral. Gramps didn't say much, nor did I see him cry. That's just how my grandfather is. After some passing years, I was traveling within Thailand when I called my grandfather to ask how he was doing, and he ranted to me about how he asked my brother, Payton a very simple request. When Payton had graduated from high school, a lot of people showed up in support of his achievement and to wish him a fair congratulation after the ceremony. Grampa's request was simple, "I'm buying you envelopes and stamps with addresses for you, so that you can write to everyone that showed up and tell them that you appreciated their efforts in coming to see you."

Payton agreed to this, but after some weeks, no one received any letters. Grampa called to inquire about an update to the letters but Payton nonchalantly, not by any ill-intention, accidentally threw the envelopes and stamps away during the move-out of the house where my mom and brothers stayed.

My grandfather on the phone was furious, and said, "How could he have been so inconsiderate?" I tried to console my grandfather through an attempt of trying to formulate some better reason as to why Payton would have thrown the cards away, it wasn't like him to do something like that. My grandfather in his rebuttal recalled when great-grandpa was still alive, and said, "You did the same thing, Taylor! Great grandpa gave you a card every year for your birthday and Christmas, but not once did you ever tell him that you appreciated what he did or send a card back. He *never* forgot about you, but he never even got so much as a 'Thank you.'"

I sat in silence on the other end of the phone line, listening intently and unsure of what to say. A weight in my chest of abrupt realization of selfishness exploded within me.

Gramps continued, "...I haven't even gotten anything from *you*. After all I do for your mom and you boys, not once have I ever even gotten so much as a letter, and that was all I hoped even great-grandpa would get. Am I to believe that I am supposed to provide for my grandkids but have them forget about me for things as small as a card, only to ask for more? Fuck that!"

I sat dumbfounded in my seat, gob smacked into a disbelief of how my Grampa felt, something that I and Payton now made him feel. I was shocked at the amount of effort that my grandfather has put into ensuring my mom and my brothers were capable of living a healthy life. If it wasn't for Gramps, I would have a hole where a positive role-model for me should have been, and who knows where I would have ended up through the struggles of my youth.

It took me aback, and I was unsure how to respond, but one thing for sure occurred inside of me that day, I would prove my love to those that I truly care about by making the efforts of showing the kind of appreciation I have for them, even if it is as small as a mailed letter or card recorded by my own hand and penmanship. These small tokens of love resonate beyond the card itself, and as I've come to learn, shows the warmth of the love provided when taken the time to bring thoughts to paper about the ones you care about.

You must do so while you can. As I have spoken about earlier in the chapters, you never know when something you say or do to someone has tremendous effects on them that might never be acknowledged. That includes negative effects as well. As my Grampa is never one to complain about many things, hearing this from him, a man that I respect, cherish, and love deeply was troubling and surprising. From someone that loves him, I wanted him to know that everything I hold within my heart is from his guidance and mentorship of how to be a respectable man. I would always want to ensure that he feels my appreciation because of it, even if it's in a mailed envelope.

What if I never learned about how he felt and I went my entire life thinking that I made him feel like I wanted to take the time out to show my thanks, when in reality I was just selfish? Even worse, what if I learned about how he felt but decided to do nothing? How will I feel when I have to face a reality when I no longer have my grandfather?

I don't know, but in my life while I have my Grampa, the most important to me is to spend as much time as possible in showing that love, no matter how many hugs, phone calls, letters written, "I love you's" and other forms of outward expression is given as selflessly as I possibly can because of the deep foundation of what that person in my life means to me.

Taking the time out of your day to write a note, or give a phone call, or give acknowledgement to someone when something reminds you of them reassures them that your love means something.

When it comes to losing that ability forever, I wonder how many people would trade back all of the riches they have, the time they've accumulated, the experience learned, just to tell someone that is no longer with us how much they truly mean to us. It is not easy to overcome difficult losses, but we must stay persistent in not taking for granted what we have now before it's too late.

I believe that the acceptance of that reality would be easier, as a religious man, if my grandfather was religious himself; and that is something that I have wrestled with for many years. I do truly wish that he believed in Jesus, and an afterlife so that I may look forward to seeing him again. It's a hard topic to navigate and one in which I haven't brought up to him because of just how hard of a topic it is. The passing of my great aunt, Aunt Linda, showed to be easier for me because she was a devout Christian, and she loved beautifully in all ways. There is a sense of peace I have in my heart when I pray and call out to her name, having this feeling that I know she is listening to me. That bit of assurance means the absolute difference between concern, and joy.

As we are here on Earth, however, it is important to stay present rather than constantly worrying about the future. So, in the presence of today, the only way to ensure that love resides within the hearts and minds of those you show it to, is to take the time out and make sure it's known to those around you.

That goes for anyone- mom, dad, grandmas, grandpas, aunts and uncles, cousins, stepparents, brothers, sisters whoever. Within my family I want them to know that I love them as much as possible, and that being with them makes me a happier person. Whoever that is in your life, even if they are just acquaintances, give 100% of yourself if you truly care for them, as I have had to hear many times of the stories of lost friends and family members where someone says, "I wish I could tell them that I forgive them." Or "I wish I could tell them I love them just one more time." Don't set yourself up for regrets. It will be hard to lose someone regardless of the situation, but it is easier to live with the respect of yourself knowing that they transparently knew how much you loved them to begin with.

It would be a failure on behalf of our parts as capable individuals able to give love to not show it to those that might not have the same opportunities of tomorrow as you do. We don't know when our time is supposed to be, and it is a hard topic to bring up, especially to those around you that you deeply care for.

So, if we are to take advantage of the time each of us has in its fullness, we must prepare ourselves mentally, emotionally, spiritually, and with an abundance of love so that those around us know how we feel, and just how much we appreciate the company of the ones you're afraid to lose.

Your preparedness will spare you from constant worries and depression while you have the time to appreciate the things in front of you. Regardless of whatever it is that you have, a concept that I have been living by, one of my many mantras is: 'nothing lasts forever, good or bad."

All things will pass, so to enjoy the good while you have it and to rejoice in the ending of the bad, it is imperative to appreciate both while they occur, as the things in which you cannot help will come your way at one time or another. You cannot stop the rain, but you can protect the things you are concerned about from getting wet with proper course of preparedness and diligence.

Continue to think about this as not to fail in the expression of your love. Be thankful for the people and things around you, and do not become a shell of your former self from loss but learn to accept that life is never fair as it is only experiences that shape us.

CHAPTER 5

GRACEFUL FAILURES

Speaking about failures, let's get one thing straight: Failure is inevitable. In every tribulation in life, there is never a guarantee of success, no matter how sure one could be of their probability for it. Sometimes, the reality is that you are destined to fail, but it might be a necessity. Think about the countless times you have experienced failure in your life so far, however, and concentrate on the difference between the times that you had failed, but continued to strive for your goals, or the moment you gave up, never to try again.

Failure may be painful, and it might come into your life at the most inconvenient times that test your grit and character to the essence of the purest degree. That's what it's meant for. Failure teaches pain, and pain either forges resilience, or weakness. You have two paths to choose at any point in your life, and it is up to you to put forth the best of yourself to come out on the other end exponentially better than before, as you will have been tempered by the failure that drives motivation.

At the end of the day, you will be beat down, until mud is smeared into your face and the bitter sand crunches against your teeth, knees and hands bloody. You will face the obstacles and opponents mocking you, disbelieving that you have what it takes to stand up, but that truly is all that it takes. Stand Up- One. More. Time.

The one who truly fails, is the one who accepts defeat. If you continue, over and over, to rise to your feet no matter how much you have been knocked down, each time you rise you build something within yourself better than you were the last time you had failed to keep your balance. I believe this comes from the inherent desire in ourselves as resilient human beings to constantly destroy the things that make us vulnerable. There is a point within all of us that will eventually refuse to allow the punches to be pulled, and we will find that we are capable of enduring terrible things, but it takes the redirection of the stumbles and pain within us to overcome all failures, and to never accept defeat.

The most successful people in our world all throughout history were not immediate victors. The men and women that contributed incredible inventions, scientific advancements, societal improvements, and inspiration for generations share similar testimonies about the power of never giving up and coming back to rock the entire world.

Think of the most famous US president in American history. I would argue that the most influential within the continental United States was none other than President Abraham Lincoln. Do you know just how much Lincoln had failed in his life? Either due to just circumstance or misfortune, Lincoln faced many challenges that tested his resolve within himself.

Lincoln was involved within the Illinois militia serving initially as a captain within the regiment, until the unit was no longer needed as the men decided they had more important obligations to family and household. Overnight, Lincoln was no longer bearing any rank. When he enlisted in a secondary militia, the new unit already had a command structure, so he enlisted within the new unit as a private! The lowest of the lowest rank, after having been honored and elected by his men in his previous militia as a commander of the men he served with.

For most, especially in today's world, if a captain got demoted to private, most would take their life to be over, and see no point in continuing on, but not Lincoln. His exemplary spirit shows the resolve of a man capable of believing in the process, as we all should. Lincoln, being self-taught in education, also failed numerous businesses, even going bankrupt twice and lost every single election he ran in- 26 to be exact, except one. All of this, but it only took one victory to show the incredible efforts of a man intolerable to defeat.

Lincoln would go on to win the election, the war, the country, and the hearts and minds of Americans almost 150 years later. Does that not resonate with you? Look at how incredible the outcome is when you look at all you have to achieve, instead of what there is to lose. Lincoln was not afraid to lose, as he was willing to sacrifice it all to accomplish what he believed in. He could have been a speck in the past as a poor president who died while serving a term during the height of a distant war, but Lincoln showed the type of person that he was, and lives within us as the best president voted by the American people and historians.

We must relate ourselves to those that have failed miserably, but redeemed their spirits in the belief that nothing could stand in their way of success; no matter how much they have failed. As we know already it is only when you accept defeat that failure is reality. As long as you have to courage to stare your opponents in the eyes and attempt to rise, no power can keep you down.

That being said, how do we fail with grace? Is it not difficult enough to look at ourselves after our stumbles and feel that we could have been smarter, wiser, more aware, or better protective of the things that you had lost? The truth is those self-reflections are the real moments where you guarantee yourself that those mistakes will *never* be repeated. This is why failure *is* important. We have all heard about learning something the "hard" way, but the truth is, unless you want something to stick with you for your entire life, the hard way is the only way.

When internal pain erupts inside of you from the realizations of the things you had failed to protect or create, the struggle within yourself will stick with you while you come to terms about how you will better approach the situation the next time you come across it in the future, as a wiser and more experienced student in the world.

Nothing is guaranteed but that we will all die in the end, so why would you not tackle each opportunity to make the best of what you can regardless of what you do. It's cynical, but it is the truth. If you believe that the price of learning to live is too great to pay now, just wait until you get the bill for regret. Don't find yourself looking back on wishing for what you could have achieved, as opposed to the things you've achieved because you learned from your failures. Life offers more than regret; recognize it before it's too late to make changes.

I fought with my mother many times throughout my life. As a hard-headed and arrogant person always searching for his independence, my mom and I bumped heads at many times within the growth of my adolescent years. It was difficult enough as well through the constant moving due to the houses that were always rented, and it became apparent that we could only settle into a place for a few years until it was time to change environments once again.

The consistent shifts of living arrangements really kept us on edge in regard to the comfort we probably needed, and the ebb and flow of spacious to cramped houses and apartments really drove a wedge into privacy and consideration for one another. My mother, in her attempt to raise three boys also needed the support, but

LOST IN LOVE | 63

because of a plethora of reasons, relationships would last for some time, but eventually fade, causing attachment to role-models we sought as father figures to disappear leaving a hole in the house for financial assistance and long-term responsibility.

Overall, as the oldest son within the house, I had a duty to ensure the proper order within the household was maintained, but as I got older, I wanted to live for myself. I believed that if my responsibilities within the house were to be a young adult, then I should be capable of making adult decisions. Of course, there were flaws in my logic that led to disagreements between my mother and I, but overall, the reality was within who I was as a person. I am independent, and I desired to make something of myself without the authoritarianism I believed was attempting to control every aspect of my life.

One day a massive argument broke out between my mother and me. This was a pattern within an entire week that had led up to a catastrophic argument between the both of us that shook walls like an earthquake. At this point, the mediator of the situation, my grandfather, gave me the ultimatum that I believe began the process of making me the man I wanted to be, and who I am today.

He said to me, "Taylor, you cannot continue to argue with your mom like this anymore. You are old enough to want to make your own decisions, and you're not going to continue to fight with the woman who shelters you. You have two options. Option one: you will leave Florida and move in with your dad in Louisiana, or option two: you will find a place of your own here, but you will not stay with your mom. I'm giving you 3 weeks find a place and move, but afterwards you cannot stay here."

When I initially heard this, I was quite floored. The prospect of having the one person whom I needed as my mediator in overcoming these challenges, the man willingly taking responsibility as almost a therapist for the family has now decided to give me the ultimatum. I didn't know what to think about it at the time.

I couldn't leave for Louisiana with my dad. As much as I loved him I had too many responsibilities in Florida. For one, I was taking classes at the local state college, for two, at the time I had my girlfriend that I couldn't leave and for three, I genuinely felt that the opportunity here was better than what I would find in Louisiana, with all due respect to my upbringing.

Filled with spite, however, I wanted to prove to the entire family that I had what it took to show just how capable I was on my own. I turned three weeks into three days and after finding one of the luckiest living situations I could have run into from an ad on no other place other than Craigslist, I purchased a U-haul and began moving the minor belongings out of my single bedroom and into a new house with three other roommates.

The situation was not glamorous, but it got the job done, and within that time of moving out, I had no car, no money, and I was still managing to make it to class every day. I knew I needed a long-term job, and so I applied for a campus security position so that I could attend classes during the day and then work the 3-11pm shift afterwards. It became glimmer of hope within the prospects of making it on my own. I took a bus to and from work and returned late in the night.

My grandfather seeing the effort I was making to uphold my independence felt pity for me, and I thank him for that. His actions of love conveyed pride and compassion that since growing up, I have attempted to imitate time and time again. He is the personification of tough love when needed, but all the while is tender and selfless. He surprised me with a car one day, and he instilled the lessons I have learned about harboring the most out of what I can strive for and appreciating what I have. My hard work and achievements were proof that he would assist me, as he knew that I wouldn't squander the opportunity to bust my ass.

At the time of writing this book, I still drive that car. A 2010 Nissan Altima, a car now at this point is thirteen years old and of which I care for as if it is my own baby and brand new, regardless of the sunspots, the chipped paint, and the occasional mechanical issues. It takes me where I need to go, but most importantly it is a sign for me that lessons learned hard are the best lessons learned out of all. (It ended up flooded by Hurricane Milton, 2024)

Because of the tough love given from my grandfather, but the overwhelming grace of his love when seeing my desperate passion to succeed, I have been able to instill in myself a sense of pride in the work I do. I managed to graduate from that state college with my associate degree and looked up in opportunities to take me to the next step.

Since I grew up with no money, I actually never considered the option of university. When I had graduated from Daytona State College, I figured that was the end of the road in terms of education for me, and I would find a place to settle into. I felt, though, that there truly was more to what I could possibly achieve, and it wasn't until I went across the street to grab some coffee at Dunkin' Donuts that I noticed a sign in the door of a near vacant office that said, "Army National Guard".

I sipped my coffee and pondered within the window of the empty office for a moment, wondering about the possibility of attempting to join the military again. The problem was, I was previously sworn in for the Marine Corps years prior, but I had unfortunately been involved in an accident while sparring in my martial arts class that resulted in a broken wrist. I needed surgery and it took months to recover, all the while I was supposed to ship out days before my scheduled surgery, and I just couldn't go.

By the time I stared into the window of the Army National Guard office, holding an AA degree to my name, the cogs began to turn, and I found myself plotting methods to ensure an enlistment into the National Guard. A few weeks after research and talking to doctors to get every possible medical document necessary for my enlistment, I waltzed into the office with commitment and the poor recruiter that had to handle the textbook size folder of medical paperwork, Staff Sergeant Dalton, God bless him, had to scan every sheet one by one to copy and upload into the computer.

My persistence showed time and time again, not allowing challenges stand before me in dissuading me from joining the military. It really was the only other option I had, since I had absolutely no method to pay for a university degree otherwise. You realize that when you literally have nothing else to lose, the will of an individual with everything to gain is the strongest of motivators in the world. Eventually, after months of work back and forth, I was enlisted into the Army National Guard and packed my entire life that could fit into an 8x10 storage unit away while I shipped to Fort Jackson, South Carolina for basic training.

Before I left, I had Hail Mary'd a single application to the University of Florida, the only application to a university I ever submitted. I clicked 'send' and forgot about the entire ordeal as I underwent the process of my head being shaved and a uniform issued. The military would own me 24/7 for the next few months until I would graduate from basic training and Advanced Individual Training (AIT).

It wasn't until after all that time that when I returned home there was an orange and blue package waiting for me at my mother's address. Big letters "UF" were plastered on one side and an edited photo of the Century Tower was laden on the back side, signifying the pride of the Gators. I hastily opened that package and found that I, to my absolute surprise, was accepted and was able to start the semester as a transfer student in person.

All of the excitement escaped me when I realized as I held the envelope and acceptance letter in my hand that I had only *one week* until the start of the semester! I had just got home, still was readjusting to finally being back at my mother's house with all items in a storage unit. With persistence, I eventually found a place to move into with my ex-girlfriend Rosana, who had also been accepted into the university as well. With just days to spare before the start of the semester we managed to completely transition to a life of full-time university students.

Two years later, after going through a break-up, a move into a new place, and broader scope on life, I am facing the end of my tenure of my undergraduate experience at the University of Florida, with potential to pursue my master's as well. As I look back at the journey, I am realizing just how much persistence and belief in oneself is required in order to overcome the challenges that you can face. I have been incredibly fortunate for the outcome that has shaped my heart to look at things in a positive sphere instead of holding animosity to the things in which I couldn't achieve, which so far, would never hold weight for keeping me down.

You must do the same. Challenges are designed intricately in ways that a patient mind and a passionate heart can withstand the winds of the worst of storms. We are designed to solve problems with more than one solution, and it is possible to believe that a failed attempt at solving those problems means that there is little hope for all else, but Thomas Edison is famous for having said about failure of all the times he attempted to make the lightbulb, "I have not failed 10,000 times, I have not failed once. I have succeeded in proving that those 10,000 ways will not work."

Consider yourself Edison and utilize your brilliant mind to challenge the status quo of that which you believe is the solution and continue to try again and again until you are certain that whatever you are doing is working in the best capacity in can.

Perhaps it may not be perfect, but the first step is to hone into your determination for success and knowing that there is no limit to what you are capable of achieving if your heart is able to withstand the long-term duration of disappointment. I promise you, though, that the success when you finally reach it in the end will pay off greater than any freely given and achievable goal.

Failing with grace is about welcoming the idea that it will happen, but turning the misfortunate in what you may experience into opportunity to learn and create better your circumstances. This derives from loving yourself. As long as you continue to love yourself, no amount of failure will ever push you to accepting defeat. To want the best for what you are trying to achieve, as well as what you would like to be for others, you must prove to yourself that you are capable of loving who you are regardless of how many times failure may attempt to ascertain doubt within you.

There is a plan for everything you do, and it is a guarantee that you will stumble, that you will fall, that you will get hurt and even feel discarded. It's unfortunate that we must endure such things, but if it is inevitable that we will experience them, then why attempt to change what we already know may occur when we undertake new challenges. It's even worse the pain when you refused to start the challenge in the first place, but that pain comes into play in the future, and you may not realize it until it's too late.

Instead of trying to change the possibilities of what can happen, focus on how you can change your reaction to that which has happened. It is never certain that what you do will turn out exactly as you intend, so the best thing you can do is be prepared to approach the uncertainty of life with an open mind and preparedness to adapt as quickly as you can. Your future self will appreciate you for thinking about reactions to uncertainties instead of trying to change them, and that will lead to a successful mindset to gradually adopt new methods of learning and understanding.

Don't give up. You can do it.

CHAPTER 6

WALK IN UNISON

"I'm sorry, I just don't love you anymore." I said quietly in my living room in front of my then girlfriend, Rosana. Months, if not years of stress and being less of a man I should have been because of an inability to work on my own personal attributes caused the separation of myself and high-school sweetheart.

I had been neglectful of my relationship, and looked to only achieve a higher ground to proving that what I was feeling was more important than how she felt. I was concerned more with my self-perseverance than quieting my thoughts and loudmouth. This continual action of selfishness caused me to speak more than I listened, and overlooked the truth of what the reality was; in which we both wanted to be happy. We both wanted a good life and to remove stress from our lives. At this point, we had been together coming up on five years. We had accomplished so much together- graduating high school and state college, joining the Army, getting accepted to the University of Florida, and traveling around the US and the world experiencing those monumental moments together as a striving couple should.

The reality was, however, is that I had grown complacent in the relationship, and complacency kills. I didn't dive myself into the truths of the detrimental traits of a failing relationship even though they were in front of me the entire time. I was attempting in any way possible to get my personal ailments heard as opposed to listening to what issues were possible to be overcome together. The rifts and distance between us were wedges of selfishness and perhaps resentment over a rotational experience of fight and makeup. This is a common occurrence upon many in the world every day, where they are more concerned with their own well-being instead of the wellbeing of both people as a unit.

I look back now, and I think, "How many times could I have gone about this situation a different way if I had approached it from a perspective of love, and wanted to reach the same goal as a team, instead of in a game of offender/defender?"

A beautiful message in scripture resonated with me as I read it, "Can two people walk together if they cannot agree on a direction?" That was my downfall. It wasn't even the act of walking in the direction, I was just unwilling to give the thought of a direction different than my own a chance, and when two people are continually arguing over the path to take, let alone the destination, there cannot be union.

How can two people walk together if a direction is not agreed upon? This question has resonated with me, and the logical part of me now looks at the reality of what along the path are we both interested in pursuing, whether it be positive or negative. Regardless of the path, there will always be something worth walking for, but the option should weigh in the negative for a decision to be made. It has been apparent to me that instead of constantly vouching for your own decisions, find between the both of you exactly what there is that can benefit both parties. More times than not, beneath the surface of disagreement is the reality that both of you are reaching the same goal and conclusion.

Silence the voice in your head that only wants to hear the other person admit that you are right. You must become humble. Approach the conclusion with love, and do not attempt to place yourself higher than the other, as the only way to convince them that you are right is by letting them know that you are in fact wanting the same comfort and happiness as they do.

Arguments and disagreements are bound to happen, and it is not always guaranteed that the destination and journey will conclude on similar paths. Sometimes, it is best to depart from someone or something that doesn't lead you where you need to go, but in my instance, I could have gone about the approach much differently than I did. I could have resonated what I wanted in a positive way that also exalted how my partner at the time also desired.

Instead, I chose to give up. I walked away from something that I was comfortable with and *could* have been redeemable if I started with the advice, I gave you in the earlier chapter- start with overcoming the small challenges of changing the things that could eventually aid in tackling the bigger issues.

I was lazy, though. I looked for the easy way out of the relationship because I didn't want to put forth the effort of improving the things in my life that caused complications between us. I felt that there was no way something that we had both worked on for so long was capable of dissipating into something that would make us passing strangers. The truth, though, is that it was easier than expected. Once I told her that I no longer loved her, the cogs in her head began to turn, and my mistake was that I had given in to accepting how I felt as defeat.

There was no coming back from what I said, and over the course of the last few months together, her disconnect allowed her to pursue the happiness that she truly wanted from me but could never achieve from someone too focused on themselves. I didn't realize how far away her disconnect had brought her until after she returned from a study abroad, and by that point, the minimization of stress and concern over a relationship freed her from further worry. Man, if only I had loved those that cared about me as much as I loved myself.

Albeit, even though it was a difficult transition, it also brought a complete change to me as well. Throughout the relationship, I had voices in my ear about how being weighed down by a relationship takes away the adventurous spirit I have naturally within me, as I was anchored by the life at home with someone I cared about.

When the relationship finally ended, I didn't waste any time to take it upon myself to escape the realms I have been so accustomed to, and I dove into the adventure of escaping what I know to travel the world. I took off that first year and traveled twice to Peru following the separation. The eye-opening experiences of what it was like to experience what I had always dreamt of was like a sudden rush of life that filled my spirit. When I started connecting with people of other cultures, other experiences, other livelihoods, I realized just how important it is to silence my own mouth and learn how to learn!

I came to understand how important it was to truly remove myself from the experiences of what I was so comfortable with and place myself in the shoes of others that have valuable lessons to share. These lessons come from the most unsuspecting people, and if you're too busy talking, then you'll pass up on incredible knowledge.

It has taught me how to look at differences in people's lives closely, and instead of reverting to what I know, I make it a valued challenge to see how open-minded my approach to others' differences can be and whether I can learn anything from it. If I had learned this in my naïve youth, then perhaps I would have less arguments, less burned bridges, less crippled relationships and a closer bond to those in approaching those differences with love in mind, regardless of who it is.

I can't go back and change the past, none of us can. The only thing we can do is look at the examples of the things that have occurred to us and make a decision. Do we choose to walk a path of adversity by only looking at the negatives in whatever direction we may walk; or do we look at what there is to gain from hard decisions to constantly make the most out of any hand we've been dealt?

The choice is ultimately yours to make, but guaranteed the heart inside of you chooses to not be consistently hurt by inconvenience. Not all things are within your control, but what you can control is how you react and how you understand the things that come your way.

Even if you deal with a particularly difficult person who is not on the same field of thinking when it comes to love, eventually your patience and passion of understanding will cause a reconsideration of action as you set the example and setting guidelines to *how* you want to settle differences.

Ultimately, communication is key, and with proper communication, you hold the master key to the hardest of locks. Most people dive directly into an argument with emotions pent up from other stresses, and it's easy to take the brunt of the emotions and push it onto the only person you can trust to be vulnerable in your emotions to, but they may take your vulnerability personally because you have not set boundaries for yourself. Communicating how to settle your differences during an argument is just as important as making the argument itself. If your intent is to persuade the other party to look at your perspective, how would yelling at them, blaming them, ostracizing or criticizing them convince them to work with you on your team to win the game?

It is imperative to approach these things with poise and humility, while also maintaining a strong position in how you feel but with an open mind. You cannot see the beauty of nature outside of a window unless you make the choice to open the shutters. Opening the shutters to see what someone else is seeing is your choice to change that preconceived image of what is outside. Ultimately, the truth of what is, can be completely unexpected once you've become ready to accept the difference.

Listen more than you speak and find the meaning between spoken words. Try not to assume, try to feel. And in the best-case scenario, your skills of communicating will allow your ability to overcome challenges by saying, "I believe you are saying..." or "I may be wrong, and correct me if I am, but I believe what you are trying to say is..."

This method of regurgitating information shows that you are indeed listening, and considering what they are talking about as serious and worth putting your attention to. All it takes is an inviting conversation deriving from love that can make someone's stress and struggles feel like they are equally as important to you as they are to them. We must do this as a way to ensure the values of what we believe are heard, but we must be receptive to those that want the same.

We shouldn't be so quick to cause disagreements or divulge ourselves to anger. There is passion that can be misguided, and negative emotions that can be misplaced onto those that intend to help us. We should be open to seeing the perspective of others for the better of everyone's world, since we're so used to living in a very personal, narrow-minded view. We should maintain an open presence and invite those that need guidance and gift it to them, as you were before you sought the knowledge yourself.

Too often do we find ourselves as defensive warriors, guarding our honor and blockading the gates to our castle inside. On the inside, the castle is represented by our heart, and we feel as though we must protect it at all costs. We tend to believe that the person we should be loving is actually like an opposing kingdom that you should be wary of, and so you protect your assets, your emotions, from them.

Once they are at our gates, and they plead with you to let them in so that they may talk about coming to an agreement cordially, you raise your weapons. You want to argue your point from outside the castle walls, but it is important to realize that you can only come to an agreement by opening up your gates and inviting them into your heart.

You as a king or queen may not be ready to relinquish full control over your own kingdom by facing those failures that caused the kingdoms to convene first, and so you attack. Through arguments and disagreements, further driving a wedge, eventually they will breach your kingdom walls, but instead of having been invited in to settle differences as diplomatic kingdoms, your heart is stormed by the thoughts and emotions brought about by an opposing force, that at one point was as equally on your side as you were to yourself.

We mustn't let our walls be breached but recognize an opportunity for both kingdoms to benefit equally from working together. As we go through our lives and continue to build relationships to kingdoms surrounding us, the old saying of, "pick your battles," becomes an important role as rulers of our own hearts to come out as a righteous and noble person in charge of all you can control.

There will be difficulties, and there will be problems that will arise, and sometimes it may seem that love is not the answer, but it doesn't matter how mad you are, aren't you mad because you love them? Aren't you upset at them because you love them? Don't you want to keep them close to you, and the emotions you feel on behalf of someone else is because of the feelings of trying to protect, care, nurture, give and provide?

You feel these things because we are encouraged to love by a great design caused by divinity. We are told to forgive those that have wronged us because it comes from the heart of love. It's written to "Turn the other cheek!"

How?! How could you turn the cheek to those who struck you, that caused you pain, that ruined something great? By love. And the more you love yourself, the less likely someone who strikes you will retain the scars in your head, in your heart, festering inside of you as you've come to realize that people are going through life just as you are, and it is their first time as well. They may not seek truth, happiness, or love, but by providing yourself a way of personal gratification and humility in understanding others, love is unbeatable, and undeniable.

CHAPTER 7

ESCAPING COMFORT

It is difficult in the beginning to understand the beauty in sacrificing comfort by forcing ourselves to remove what we are used to. However, once we have opened the door to uncertainty, the possibilities of great success or great risks grow exponentially. To mitigate the risks, proper research and knowledge about the goals achievable should be made perfectly clear with yourself. Backup plans and different avenues of approach may not cover an exact fallback for every situation, but it does provide an umbrella of ideas that could assist you given a worst-case scenario. The importance of research in your plans will come back to bless you in times of trouble once you've decided to remove the confining safety barriers of comfortability.

Comfort is a dynamic feeling. We often limit actions that are necessary for growth because of the feeling of complacency derived from comfort. It's a feeling that provides a false sense of gratification once you've stayed on a level long enough to fear losing where you stand. You may run in circles willing to sacrifice just enough to be comfortable, but as long as comfort binds your heart, and the fear of losing surrounds you, the action of overcoming these challenges will eventually no longer bring satisfaction in life, but a regret that you didn't aim higher.

It is possible to get cold feet and believe that aiming for a higher level may cost you the price of what you've already gained. If you hadn't brought yourself to understanding the commitment and work that went into getting where you were at in the first place, then of course there would be no reason to fear further losing the placement you struggled to achieve.

Have you ever accomplished a great feat, having poured your heart and soul into achieving it, only to end up realizing that you're holding onto that moment for as long as you could with no further progression? There is a fear of the loss and hoping that you don't backslide into the struggles of being where you were before you became successful. Do you remember when that feeling of success was new, and you thought that you would never give up the ground you earned to go back to what it was like before? Or perhaps, once you've reached that point of success where your motivation to continue striving for greater success diminishes and comfort overcomes your drive. The doubt for those achievements turning into a colossal failure seizes the hearts of those looking to shoot for the stars but enjoy the complacency of viewing them from a telescope.

One must look over the edge of uncertainty and put faith in the best possible outcome. It may not go the way as expected, but the knowledge and experience gained from taking the leap of faith may lead you to appreciating that which you have, but at the same time can teach about methods that don't work versus those that do in reaching desirable goals. Make a list of goals you are intending to achieve and ensure that those goals are incrementally achievable the higher you go on your list.

The highest goal may be something that seems unattainable at the time of writing, but the steppingstones of progress build walkways of overcoming the impossible. Having a continual set of goals also bring your complacency to a minimal grasp upon your spirit, as you will know that you have not completed your goals and will hold yourself to that feeling of regret if you don't submit yourself to the slight, continual effort required.

I have lived by a philosophy while I travel overseas to indicate the power of how comfort distorts perception. In my home, I usually keep a semi-uncomfortable mattress for my everyday needs. I try to avoid buying the high end, ultra-comfy mattresses that you just sink into, because the most I have ever heard people talk about when they get homesick is, "I miss my bed." It was a revelation to me that has worked so far, that if my bed is negligible in competition with other mattresses or choices to sleep on, then I will never compare where I sleep to my bed back home, and that has helped me reduce my homesickness while away. That openness has allowed me to choose couches, mats, pullouts, hammocks, tents, straw or cotton mattresses and others and I have never had a moment where I thought, "Man, I really wish I was in my own bed right now." That has helped me tremendously in relying on my comfort for making decisions on where I should stay, for example.

In further personal experience, I was faced with an unnerving desire to escape the world I was familiar with and knew. Within me, after years of language study, I wanted to grab ahold of the globe, and vagabond my way across uncertain journeys that would lead me to personal growth and love in its entirety for that which I previously had never known. I understood I could immerse myself within the cultures abroad and harness the energy of what motivated me to challenge my grit and character.

It wasn't until after my long-term relationship ended that I was able to break free the chain of comfort and consistency to consider only myself on an adventure of uncertainty. My first solo-travel experience was by circumstance, not desire. I had invited two close friends to join me for a planned guys' trip. Of course, though, even though there was a 3-month head start on planning, I found myself as the only person at the airport ready to board a flight to Lima, Peru.

Imagine if I had been too afraid to go on with the trip, all because of my friends being unable to join me, and I decided to wait until they could. By God, I know I would have waited for an eternity- all respect to my boys. Within this is a valuable lesson to learn and take away from the story- as long as you're waiting for someone else, you can never live for yourself. The right people will arrive and leave when they are required to do so. Whether the separation is hard or not, the truth is that the unempirical evidence suggests whatever happened, was, is, and will be a canon event. You cannot change the future and events that are bound to happen, you can only change your reaction to them.

With that thought process, it matters most that you are capable of looking into the potential of what is achievable through your own actions. With the removal of expectations on my very first trip, I found myself alone on a flight to South America with zero knowledge or concerns about what would occur during my initial duration of 25 days. I landed into the Jorge Chávez International Airport at 11:30pm after a surprisingly short 5-hour flight from Fort Lauderdale and met face to face with swindlers and taxi-scams that I wasn't aware of at the time and paid initially 20x higher than locals should-my first mistake.

I ended up running into obstacle after obstacle and didn't realize where or what I had gotten myself into. With a massive 60L backpack, a beige Tilley hat and a truly gringo complexion walking around at 1am finding a hotel to crash in for the night, to say I looked as if I didn't belong was an understatement. I wasn't within the tourist zones, no, I was directly in the city center of La Victoria, which at the time, I wasn't aware was one of the more dangerous areas in Lima, Peru.

Through luck, I was placed upstairs in an aged and old-timey "hotel" last minute to get some sleep. The hotel, which had rooms that were basically what you would imagine to be found inside of a monastery, with a single bed, hardwood floors, and since in South America, no A/C or heat. Luckily there was a nice little bathroom with an inviting shower that I truly needed after the duration aboard the flight and being in an airport for close to 14 hours.

Regardless of what I believed about the hotel at the time, with no preparation, I was lucky to find a place to sleep for the night. The uncertainty of whether I would find a bed to lay my head would follow me throughout every night, because I never knew where I would find myself due to my spontaneity. Luckily, the affable nature of my character meant I never went without pleasant company.

That first day, I woke up to bustling sounds of car horns and traffic jams, people yelling in Spanish, and vendors announcing their new inventory. It was only when I opened up the window to the outside that the most beautiful sight of a city had come to life, and there I was directly in the middle of it observing from my second story window as I ate an apple for breakfast. There was a sporadic flood of oncoming traffic from all directions and caught directly within the centers of the kaleidoscopic nature of the intensely colored buildings, the smell of local made delectables in the forms of ready-to-eat street food, I realized that I had made it. Beyond all expectations or assumptions, concerns or anxiety, I was there, and in the presence of my disbelief, was an unforeseen and surprising serenity. I was alone, able to make my travels my very own personal reality however I saw fit.

I had no one to tell me when to wake up, where to go, who to see, what to do, and my absolute freedom allowed my free-roaming soul to wander absolutely in any possible direction. I checked out from my last-minute hospitable hotel and in true gringo fashion, walked the busy streets of La Victoria to grab breakfast and headed to the Plaza de Las Armas in Lima to secure a SIM card and coffee.

I stopped at a small café and saw someone who was not of native complexion to Peru, and I spoke English to him. He looked up at me and he kind of laughed, amused by the obvious nature of my foreignness. I told him with desperation that I needed to find a place to activate a SIM card. He told me he would help me, and through a quick introduction, named himself as Paulo from France.

Paulo was an incredible person to have met, as he brought me directly to the Moviestar shop (a Verizon or ATT equivalent to Peru) to activate my Peruvian SIM. I thought without him, I would have been incredibly stuck without knowledge of how to conduct myself within the first hours of survival within this foreign country. It was hard enough to get directions to the Plaza de Las Armas anyway, especially since I had to walk due to not having any GPS and needed to map out the city center from my hotel before I left.

I thanked him tremendously, and invited him out to accompany me, but he said that he was leaving that day from Lima to head to other cities in Peru. I shook his hand and got his contact information and bid him farewell as we agreed we could meet up again. We parted ways without a second thought, and that was the beginning of my consistency of saying goodbye to good friends.

Throughout the time backpacking my way across the beaches, deserts, oases, mountain ranges, open fields, urban and rural retreats, sheer luck came during a hike up an immense sand dune overlooking Huacachina. As I was preparing to set out for the adventure that day from the Wild Rover Hostel in Huacachina, a familiar face passed by me and called out my name. Surprised as hell, none other than Paulo himself stood before me, having traversed other areas around Peru, found both of us within the same hostel, in the same town, preparing to set out on a whirlwind adventure.

Him and I spent the entire day together, made friends with some Irish gals, and sped across desert sands in dune buggies, hiked the incredible dunes circling the desert oasis as if in a massive bowl, and even watched the sunset across the horizon as if we had been friends for a lifetime.

At the end of the day trip out in the sand, we sat down and discussed our lives over a refreshing bowl of fruit. The reunion was incredible, but short lived. Our next destinations brought us once again apart from each other. For a second time, I gave Paulo a hug and told him to be safe, and happy travels. He bid me a warm farewell and went our separate ways. That was the last time I saw him.

Throughout the journey, my time within Peru had unexpected turns of events, and I found myself within the presence of incredible acquaintances, experiences, and memories made to shape my very own character. With an insurmountable number of challenges that I had faced, not once did I doubt my abilities. The freedom to overcome the difficulties I faced while pursuing greater knowledge of Peruvian culture brought me to harvesting within myself a feeling of incredible joy and love for the connections I made.

Within the same year, I had returned to Peru twice. With complications of being robbed, Peruvian protests of December 2022, difficulties in transportation, sickness, missing flights and more, the negatives never overburdened the feeling of freedom and knowledge to gain. The desire for the sporadic and spontaneous amount of people I could meet overcame the feeling of doubt that I couldn't take something valuable away from my trip to Peru, in the hopes that I left with more than I came with.

Truly, I stepped away from South America with a powerful surge within my very bones the desire to see all of the world and connect closely and personally with cultures on all corners of our world. I realized how expansive and diverse it is, but also just how many tribulations there are to overcome with dipping your feet into the waters of adventure and getting bitten by the travel bug.

This love that I feel has translated its way to my being, and I pursue that feeling at every turn I make. Whether it be an influence on my career, education, personal goals, language journeys, or people I meet, getting out of my comfort zone has allowed the love for these things to overcome who I am, and I have accepted it as bringing myself to be the best I can in the goals I have set for myself to accomplish what I'm passionate about.

The truth is that you need to get out of there. Your life is dependent on what you have experienced. Keeping an open mind as an individual ready to accept the difficulties of the unknown will bring you to life as someone unafraid of that which you cannot help, but preparing you to become better when faced with similar instances in the future.

The overwhelming feeling that itches your soul when desiring to achieve the unthinkable, is the remnant of the dreams from youth, which is the last defense from the voice within your head that others managed to convince that your dreams were improbable.

People will continually attempt to convince you otherwise that your dreams are unfathomable, or it is too dangerous, or the means in which you believe is possible could never be. I don't have the answer as to why the ideas from others tend to be pessimistic. I don't have an answer how so many people can look back and wish they had done more for themselves but attempt to sway others from accomplishing that which they couldn't.

The single most important thing anyone can do, now that I have learned, is to ensure that whatever decision you make- if possible- can be thoroughly researched. Knowledge is power, and in a world of readily available knowledge, secrets aren't so well hidden if only one knows where to look. I tend often to reference YouTube, or what I like to call it- YouTube University. With thousands of people that have done exactly as you want to do, to believe that any answer could be found from others sharing their disparities is a fallacy. Learn from them and make better the circumstances you are able to avoid.

Sometimes though, you're going to be completely unprepared. You might find yourself looking down at the barrel of a gun like I did in Miraflores. You can't prepare for something like that completely, but you can take precautionary measures that ensure that your safety, plus the safety of important belongings that can be accounted for with backup plans.

I won't lie, life can be scary. Anyone that has ever lived can tell you this. How far, though, are you willing to go to accomplish the unthinkable? Do the risks of what is desired outweigh the reward, or vice versa? That is a personal decision everyone should make to fulfill within them the overall satisfaction of living a life that is meant to be, not just limiting action due to fear.

Get out there, experience the colors of the world, take in the scents from bustling street markets, the smiles or glares of passing strangers, say hello to the person on the bus next to you, do something you're afraid of, share your stories and build a new you from the experiences you haven't been scared to make. Your future self will thank you for living a full life.

Encompass yourself with the love to undergo the splendors of what is yet to be discovered. Fulfill your spirit with the guidance of the voice that has long been forgotten since a young age. Do not let the pressures of the consistent should-be's define what could have been. The love for culture, the love for people, and pursuit of true compassion should propel you forward in the constant motivation to pursue what is within your grasp.

Utilize that love within yourself for the dreams wished to be seized and expand the boundaries of what it means for you to truly escape.

CHAPTER 8

HATE TO LOVE

It's quite funny how the more I have begun writing this book, the more content I have to write about. It's almost like God is saying, "Don't forget this;" or, "Here's something else you can write about." While writing, I have been under the turmoil of having to reflect deeply as to the practice of my own advice.

Knowing to do the right thing and actively executing that goodness comes from more of a proactive approach to ensure your decisions and words are appropriate for whatever situation you find yourself in. I do intend to live deeply by the words that I write before you, and I would make every attempt as to not be a hypocrite of my own advice, but it shows how hard the reality of working to be a better person in loving others can be.

I had a backsliding on the advice of my love recently, and it hurts me to admit that I have let down someone whom I cared for within my heart of hearts. This chapter is to represent the feeling of how sometimes, we hate to love, as in the sense of being vulnerable when it comes to opening ourselves to it, but also how to proactively turn the emotion of hate into love. We get hurt, we get broken down, torn from our balconies of happiness and joy; the change can be quite rapid. One minute you feel as if you are on top of the world, but the next you feel as though your knees scrape the ground as you make attempts to crawl out of the mud beneath you.

I would be remiss to say that I had lost a very special person close to me within my life. It is not every day that someone is so caring and compassionate that just having them around makes you feel stronger, smarter, and better about yourself- until they don't. My dilemma came from the mismanaging of emotions that were not derivative of the love intended, and I had submitted my emotions to that of pride and defense.

I hadn't let her into my kingdom or knocked down my walls for her because of the types of personalities we both share- independent and strong-willed individuals. Because of the similarities of our personalities, we clashed often with ideas of how things should be done.

I had many opportunities up until the point in which I had let my emotions take control of my better judgement, to improve the relations of how I dealt with the arguments with someone I supposedly cared for. In my anger I said words that I should have never said, and in saying them, to her, was so unforgivable that it was as easy as those three words that I lost the person whom I was so appreciative for in my life but gone in an instant. Those three words?

I hate you.

So pent up was I in my own frustrations during an argument that I said this, and it was a mistake I never should have made. I realized how much it affected her. After all the arguments we had in the past, all the disagreements and the differences in stances we took, there was never a problem that couldn't be solved. It was only when the boundary was pushed that would make anyone feel utterly disrespected, did things turn for the worst. Three words cost me the relationship I had with my best friend. She was one who shared dreams and ideas with me, the friend that gave time and effort to make greater adventures and to be content within each other's company, and God, did she make me laugh.

Leading up to the incident in the car with her when those words escaped my lips, and the number of encounters that I could list on one hand afterwards, the viewpoint of our ideas were never on the same page. Truthfully, it was stressful and exhausting to even hold basic conversations on both ends. Realistically, I believe there were a lot of miscommunications. It was clear that we just didn't belong as friends anymore, and it was increasingly obvious, especially after some time apart from each other and both realizing our respect levels.

I could easily say I loved her. I loved her as someone that I could never see being without in my life. Even though we weren't together, I always felt like I could count on her if I needed something and her for me. Yet, almost as bad as a breakup, losing a friend is a kicker into the teeth of your reality. It made me understand how vulnerable we are to others, and why it seems that some people, though longing for that affection, attention, and love, push others away and keep their barriers up from others who haven't been vetted truly.

I felt after two long years of knowing someone as my friend, that I was well entangled with the character of their being. I felt that I was confident in feeling as if I knew the person I had spent so much time with, and that I could handle the unexpected thrown my way. I was completely wrong. The forms of love that I give to my very small circle of incredibly close friends radiate to them like a pulsating sun. I give my warmth to those that matter most to me, as having loyal friends is more valuable and satiable than any number of followers or likes, or texts on a colored background.

When my friendship ended, I took a deep amount of time to reflect upon the boundaries that weren't respected on my behalf, and the things I did that were disrespectful to her. I realized that there were many failures in the system imposed by us that led us to never being on the same page, and always jumping into a defensive mode anytime questions or tone were misinterpreted.

It's not that I truly hated the friend I was so close with, yet it was a reaction of emotion that made it feel so real. That situation was approached from looking into the emotional side of why I was angry, instead of the loving side as to why there was a disagreement in the first place. Regardless of whoever started the argument or issues, you soon realize once the flames have died that in fact, it was ridiculous to engage an argument in the first place. Perhaps the other party wasn't aware of their tone, or the words they use, or the body language of their message. It's likely that the voices fueling your insecurities are just that—your own insecurities.

It may be the case that the other party truly becomes frustrating after voicing concerns, but the message just never seats once received. If that's the case, having the strength to respectfully remove yourself from those that disobey boundaries is a personal factor that only you can achieve. That's the case that should have occurred for me, but I'll admit that I was weak and attached too strongly to the person I was very close with for two years. It's not always easy.

I noticed after the end of our endeavors that the toxic traits that festered between us, amplified by emotion only caused greater heartache, and it took just one sentence, one tone, or one misplaced emotion to set off the time bomb between us. I sometimes think people cry out in anger solely because their love language is not being met, and it is really a calling to ask for things to be different- to be better. However, sometimes letting go will be the most important action taken, especially if you can reflect upon the mistakes and learn from them, but most importantly to forgive.

I don't know if she and I will ever talk again in our life, but through reflection, I've begun to turn that facade of hatred into love, forgiving her for the way she made me feel with the hope that she realizes the same. We may not always have the chance to let the other person know we've turned hatred to love, but it doesn't have to be for the other person. That experience can be for you alone. Once you've forgiven yourself and grown wiser, you will forgive those that have neglected you and happiness is waiting around the corner.

There is an importance in understanding that words create and harness the most of vile of emotions, but also some of the sweetest, most tender of connections; that is a power few understand and harness.

Hate is an empty feeling, devoid of life and passion in the pursuit of happiness. Yet, it is also one of the most driving and motivating factors for someone to commit actions against others in the fiercest of ways. That energy is also unequivocally destroyed with the power of love and is stronger than any other feeling. The spirit of love drives humanity to do incredible things unlike any emotion the mind and heart could be compelled to do.

Unlike hate, which is an emotion that without a doubt only brings itself to carry destruction along with it, it is commonly displayed for the purpose of taking away life, metaphorically or literally. Love, however, is the only emotion that would bring a person to give up their own life for the purpose of others, and in that case, love proves to overcome all the hate that is brought upon you.

If only I had been more aware of the emotions within my body associated with negativity, perhaps I would have been more in tune with what emotions we both were feeling instead of solely focused on my own. My approach with love could have given me patience, and I would have watched what words came out because of those feelings.

Those that have been hurt in the past are quick to hate love. We justify our actions of distancing compassion by building a barrier brought about by the breaking of trust from someone we love. It's a harsh reality that our pain influences how we treat others, and how much or how little love is given to those deserving it.

The cycle of pain must be broken from past mistakes to move forward in loving those who find it difficult to accept it, or to give it.

As spoken by Oscar Wilde, "Hearts live by being wounded." To undergo the process of forging the perfect connection and friendship, or exalting the love between two people, the realization that all things, good or bad will end at some point or another is imperative. Whether distance, or emotions, actions, time, or death we all will find ourselves at a loss. Enjoying the times that are present and continuing to plan for the future is necessary to procure the best possible relationship.

It is still relevant that it all may end, and sometimes rather quickly. Usually, there are enough signs to allow for preparation, but that is not always the case.

Regardless, Seneca encourages the best out of those that pursue fulfillment in those close to us both present and departed:

See to it that the recollection of those whom we have lost becomes a pleasant memory to us.

Who is to say that because of problems that arose, or the arguments against each other or the tears shed should change your stance about the character of what made you gravitate towards that person in the first place? You are in control of your reality and can live within the realm of resentment, or you can make the conscious decision to accept that people and times change, and it is possible to enjoy the progress and journey even if you both were not equally yoked.

Once again, we are all learning how to love. We are all learning to become closer to the truth and understand the differences that make life so vibrantly diverse. Do not fret the losses, as becoming more in tune to love will resonate with those around you, make you perceived as a happier person, and will ultimately allow gains to come from your losses, and in my personal experience, usually for much better reasons. People make mistakes and people mess up. Sometimes the compatibility you thought you had with someone was fueled by distractions to keep you from realizing that the incompatibilities were overshadowed by emotional fondness and blindness.

I've learned that so much pain can occur, and many things may pile upon each other to create a force to be reckoned with. It will put you on your ass and kick you while you're down, but sometimes that's just the way it happens. However, once in a while, you get so tired of going it alone, that you reach out and extend yourself to someone which you take a leap of faith with. Sometimes, you find this person to be such a blessing, that they could only have been strategically placed in your life. With that person, you feel as though you can challenge the world.

This feeling is a love that goes deeper than just for companion, but it is a love within you that produces a ferocity that genuinely changes you to become better for yourself and them. I have been so honored to have experienced someone that gave so much of themselves and allowed themselves to fully place their trust in me, which I held close to my heart dearly. This experience with an amazing girl from D.C. was short, but Kailey showed me that I am truly capable of love. I realized that I am truly capable of carrying the fragility of a Fabergé egg like true trust and love that I would do everything in my power to protect it and keep it.

Perhaps it is easier to hate to love, but maybe it's worth it to take a chance, and love fully without hesitation and take a daring step onto the edge of uncertainty.

CHAPTER 9
SEPARATION OF HEARTS

Love is a passionate emotion. When love is fulfilled selflessly and the strength between two reflects that of steel, it could seem impossible for the separation of hearts -the dying flame of a once roaring fire of love- to occur. The truth is, life is never fair. We find ourselves looking back onto the memories of fantastic people that made incredible differences within our lives. We revel in the past experiences that allow us to grow and change throughout our dynamic and short times on earth.

We are lucky if we manage to maintain a lifelong partner that in a desirable essence, is a fusion of ourselves with another being that continually keeps the flame of love alive. Sometimes, however, there are other plans for both of you. The saying, "right person, wrong time" can occur with the strongest of bonds. These people whom we would sacrifice ourselves for and give all of what we are worth to keep the sanctity of love can fall short of everlasting fusion. The wicked part is that life can throw curveballs and change the course of our trajectory to separate us from that person.

The key is to realize that we are never in positions to argue fate. Ancient Stoics reflect upon the ideology of focusing what you can control, not what you can't. Do not propel yourself to avoiding change if it only amplifies the course of it. People become too inversely selfish attempting to protect themselves to preserve their love, that it pushes two people farther from the love that was present and created in bountiful abundance. The idea of soulmates is not universally recognized, in fact, some people reject the idea in its entirety. I would say, however, that there is fusion of the soul with the right person, and the outpouring of love into one that is unlike any other. In the course of that person moving on in their life, it does not take away the value of what has been gained. The purpose of what that person provides or will change in your life may not be immediately recognized, but without a doubt there will be a lesson learned, especially with the pain and heartbreak that usually comes with it. Ultimately, as we already know, time is truly the solution to healing. One factor we typically overlook is appreciating the lessons given to us instead of resenting that it happened in the first place.

Separation may not always be because of what you think it is. The unfortunate aspects of people are it is incredibly hard to be honest to ourselves, and that translates to how we express honesty to others. Human beings are purposeful in the resiliency of their flaws.

Humans act or think a certain way and claim it to be the only way. It is common for us to paint the picture of others deviating from those thoughts to be outsiders and against your way of life and thus we gravitate to those like-minded people even in error. That being said, if one cannot be completely honest with themselves, or have the inner confidence or ability to communicate how they feel they may be able to hide their true emotions for incredibly long stents of time, including years.

Eventually, humans will break under the pressure of their own stress if they are unsure how to communicate their needs, or perhaps they explode and become hostile, or maybe they find another in an act of searching for honeymoon phase thrills, something new. These actions are because of an inability to communicate, and the inability to look internally to weigh options or voice their opinions and concerns. Of course, there are two sides to every story but if one is truly to love, there is an absolute need for communication and honesty to provide positive feedback and constructive criticism that builds a partner. Even then, one could do everything right, yet it could still end unexpectedly because the person has served their purpose whether you know it or not.

Life also is a major factor. We are all living, breathing, changing and making the best of what we can. Outside factors that have no regard on the love of another is not a reason to resent or lament over loss. People need to find their happiness in all facets of the word, and perhaps one chunk in the realm of relationships is not everything that a person is looking for. These factors include work, school, distance, time away, passions, goals, or internal reflection. We cannot take someone leaving to pursue their goals personally even if it seems personal to you. It will hurt and create a heavy heart, but if you supported the dreams of someone while you had them, and you feel as though your energy was wasted, you cannot dwell on it.

You must understand that to love someone is to be there not just physically, but deeply internal and spiritually. If you turn from that person and hate their choices to the core, you can, but you should realize that for whatever purpose you served, you can make the transition easy or hard by taking it personally. Realize that you alone have gotten someone to where they are confident enough to take on new challenges. It may be a heartbreaking poison that fuels a rage, or you can toughen up, be proud that you provided all you could and find someone that deserved your effort, your time and energy. You already found that you are capable of making great change in others, so why limit your ability only because of heartbreak and separation.

All good things must end.

It is an absolute must for good things to end, because when we realize the potential for loss, we praise better the good. We cherish the good and hold it close to our hearts. It sucks to have a weight in your chest that feels like you're being held underwater gasping for a minuscule breath that keeps you from drifting deeper into cold and deep waters.

How are we supposed to condition ourselves to breathe if we've never had to fight for our breath? How do we become victorious over the weight on our chests if we've never had to lift more than what you think you can carry? Someone who can push through pain gains victory and achievement to stand on the other side of tribulation. When that knowledge is gained, it can be shared.

People can leave, and soon the only thing left will be memories. Many people get confused and can often become too drawn to the past that they are unable to avert their attention to the bigger picture in the moment, caught up in memories that blinds their conscience or potential to make a better future. Or they hold on to an old saying that causes pain in the process of longing:

If you love something, let it go. If it comes back, it's yours.

Yes, letting go of something you love for the greater good is an incredible sacrifice, but to be a lover, one must know when to lay down their arms, but also when to pick up the blade and fight for love. Often, too many are afraid to revisit the past, or the decision to return to a previous relationship. Distance and time apart from someone can foster a void for love that is susceptible to outside variables of persuasion. We also may be so afraid of the rejection of rekindling our hearts that we never make the attempt to share how we feel to each other. We must remain vigilant not to allow our emotions turn to further pain and resentment because of our offers of rekindling being declined.

It takes such nobility to push ourselves to look at an old partner that at one time defined everything about our lives and perceive them as just an experience that shaped your current self. Look back on previous heartbreak or sorrow. Visualize your past self and how much you have worked through to become greater than before. The amazing thing is that you have grown! You've become so strong to make a decision to realize each other's greater potential and to accept that just because one must go, love doesn't have to for yourself or others. Don't fall into the trap of tormenting your body and mind just because you feel self-pity or sorrow. You are better than any problem; you are greater than any loss.

It is easy to find in others unhealthy habits of distracting us from our pain. The nature of our modern world pushes for that independence and ability to live freely, separated from the demands of true love. We are bogged down with men and women within our midst upon the phones in our own pockets more times than we can count, all looking for attention- your attention. That distraction- that pursuit, to become free again and find that next "perfect one" leads you into heart break and uncertainty with what love truly is. We cannot disgrace ourselves by being driven with the mentality that just because of loss, you cannot gain. We cannot turn to drugs and alcohol expecting those vices to become the love that's missing. You set yourself up for failure every time a vice comes in to fill a hole within you. You've already learned how to love, so give your heart the healing it needs and the reflection, no matter how long until you've become confident in what's next to come. Find positive, healthy ways to express yourself and branch into directions that maybe a relationship held you back from. You only become more confident and capable for what's coming next. You must participate in life. Think of the outlets you have to your advantage (i.e., the gym, martial arts, yoga, taking dance classes, learning a new trade or craft, and the ability to meet new friends in the process of doing these things.)

Further, when one leaves, the one you shared pain with, happiness with, it's all too easy to focus on the reasons why *you* want them to stay, as opposed to why it may be important that they go. Life is full of opportunity and potential, and the reasoning behind change is often never clear in the beginning but will one day allow you to realize why throughout all of that pain, you've learned how to love and the type of love you want. A verse from the New Testament of the Bible really portrays the precedence of staying faithful in the journey:

Romans 8:18, "All of the pain you are feeling, is *nothing* compared to the joy that is coming."

Read that again. All of that pain, all of the suffering, all of the despair in the ways that life has torn you down and spit you out after flattening your spirit is absolutely NOTHING compared to the absolute joy and happiness that is coming if you stay the course, and let life and it's' time happen accordingly. Saying goodbye is one of the hardest things someone can do. It shows such maturity in the acceptance of change, but can also be a winding descent of emotion if you do not internally reflect on the goodness that comes out of that said change.

Even in my own heart, I have regrets of letting particular people go, or openly letting them walk out of my life due to uncertainty about my own future. I've let those that have expressed their absolute love to me to be let down due to my absence of emotion returned. The perpetually tiresome nature of dragging someone along through the process of figuring out oneself is not conducive to a healthy or lasting relationship, and I have broken a heart that dedicated more effort than she ever needed to, all in the hope that she could change it.

Unfortunately, the reality is only we can change our hearts, and I should have let go sooner as opposed to falsely believing that something in me would change within their presence. Then, when she finally closed that door and walked away, the passing of glances and the constant thought about wishing things were different concocted within my feelings of remorse for my actions. And while I still see her and pray that the nature of our lives was different, there is a part of me that needs to let the guilt eat at me; for it is a learning experience to never put that stress upon another, nor myself again.

Quick Tip:

Catalog your thoughts and emotions in a journal. Seriously. Having a way to share how you feel on paper allows your mind to reflect on how you truly feel inside. When you have a need to express it with a trusted person in your life, you've given your mind the opportunity to decompress the thoughts, emotions, and actions to give a truly powerful expression. In the future, you can then look back on old issues and see how much you've grown and become a more rounded, dynamic person capable of fighting tough battles and coming out victorious!

CHAPTER 10

SEARCH FOR LOVE WITHIN YOURSELF

You are a beautiful person. Look at you. Look at the lessons you've learned and how much you've grown. When you see yourself in the mirror, you should smile and rejoice in the fact that you have a reflection to look into, as so many have lost theirs way before their time.

You are a strong person with the bountiful potential to move mountains with just a bit of faith. All of what we search for in this life is to be happy and content, yet we find ourselves at the forefront of wickedness. Be the good you wish to see within this world. Love openly and fully to those in your lives and hearts that give themselves up into your hands and care for them like they are your brothers, sisters, sons and daughters.

It is often that you may run into someone of whom you feel is undeserving of kindness or love, but those people specifically have never been loved enough in their lives to truly know the difference between their world and the real one. It is the duty of us with hearts capable of empathy and understanding to turn ignorance into a learning opportunity. Some people have been brainwashed by selfish desires and personal instant gratitude, that they have forgotten how to be decent as humans in the most minute sense of the word. Be patient with them and resist the temptation to argue by attempting to convert them to your way of thinking. It won't happen through singular interactions. Change is an effect of external factors and environment to influence the internal mind and spirit through a duration of time.

Instead, focus on presenting yourself as a person of your own growth, as a reflection of your own understanding. Loving your friends and your enemies equally allow you to know both, as well as limiting surprises from either. You may find that through opposition, you handle absurdity better and are more willing to be patient with insatiable people.

Inside of you is a person that is capable of providing so much for not only yourself, but for the ones who are hurting internally who are inexperienced in expressing themselves. At the end of the day, you can be the guide that allows someone to pursue a more righteous and open-minded lifestyle through the example of your own life. You can love indiscriminately to yourself, and branch out to affect the countless others that look up to you that will remain nameless in your head.

You don't understand the power capable of being harnessed. Oh, tiny speck in the grandeur of this universe, don't you realize the power of lightning you carry within you? Can you not see that within you is an energy so great that you can bring someone to tears, or to smile? As just a small blip on the timeline of existence, look at the power within you. Your existence here on Earth is no small feat, and it is the duty to yourself to make the most out of what you can offer and provide. Success is not based solely on whether you can reach your own goals. You will fight tooth and nail to get that because it is what you want. However, are you successful enough that you can help with the goals of others? That's what you should strived for.

We all wish that we can go back to our youth, especially now that we feel that time is barreling past us faster than we can manage to keep up. COVID has eradicated the consistency in timing and thrown off the balance of normalcy that we are still recovering from. Don't let this accelerated time draw you into uncertainty and confusion. Keep your goals and continue down the path you laid for yourself. Just because COVID forced some of us to defer our plans or change our course temporarily, it cannot be the cause of our incompletion of desires. Defeat is only once you've quit.

With this passing of time, we wish we could take back the moments we've lost, and regain the potential and momentum we previously retained. If middle aged and wishing to return to the delicacy of youth at 18 years old, think instead of being 90 years old, clinging to life and about to merge into infinity. What would you have done differently right now in this moment and age that would make your 90-year-old self proud? Ponder these questions and ensure that whatever action you take each day is an acknowledgement to weaknesses, and the potential for growth.

Reflect your life, your mind, your spirit, and give unto others the love only you can provide. Love may be similar, but the love you hold is only yours. Take advantage to make a lasting mark on those fortunate enough to have been blessed by your love in an indiscriminate and unconditional way.

Be an adventurer! Go out and see the world and experience the amazing opportunities that wait in all corners of this amazing little planet. You will be surprised just how many people are willing to give this love thing a shot and connect with strangers from faraway countries, in languages neither can understand, over beers uncounted. This inherent desire within us is fueled by a step into uncertainty that buzzes about in the back of our mind and electrifies our spine to take the next steps into greatness.

Now is not the time to wait for the next break, as opportunity is gifted to those not who wait, but those who search. Henry Van Dyke said, "Some succeed because they are destined to; most succeed because they are determined to." Be determined to grow, be determined to learn, be determined to succeed- not just for yourself, but for those around you.

At the end of the day, there is a person that stands in front of a mirror, and when you look into those eyes, I hope that you see passion. I hope that you see ambition. I hope that you feel content and fulfilled with who you see before you. If not, I want you to challenge yourself, even if it is just making your bed in the morning, or sweeping the floor. Build up to feeling accomplished by putting love into your work and recognizing the pride that comes from seeing your own efforts and the small change you can make each day.

You can fulfill whatever you set your mind to with dedication and consistency. There is no guarantee that what you set your heart out for will be quick or easy, but I guarantee that one day you will look yourself in the eyes while peering into your reflection, and tell yourself with all of the heart you have, that you are proud of who you see.

I am proud of you. I love you. I hope that within your heart, you can recognize it. Go out into the world, and give yourself to others; not materialistic things. The return on your investment for the love that you give into the world will be reflected ten-fold by those that feel it and by God. It is the character essence of what we can strive to become, indiscriminate lovers of truth, humanity, and morality.

And so, when you finally lose yourself in love, it's not a gentle acceptance of fate, but a choice to be fully seen, to stand naked in all that you are, stripped of masks and defenses. This kind of love demands everything and leaves nothing hidden—it's raw, unfiltered, a fire that burns down walls and exposes the truest corners of your soul to others. You may ache, you may fall apart, but in that unraveling, you'll find a kind of peace that only love brings, a truth deeper than words, and the quiet knowing that here, in all the chaos and vulnerability, you are whole. This is where you find freedom—not by guarding your heart, but by giving it away completely. And in that surrender, you don't lose yourself— you become lost in love. You finally become everything you were meant to be; for yourself and humanity. Go out into this world, and become lost.

Questions:

What steps will you take to rediscover the love within yourself?

What have you experienced that is worth it to reflect upon and learn from?

What can you do today to show someone, even yourself, that you love them?

"Love is born into every human being; it calls back the halves of our original nature together; it tries to make one out of two and heal the wound of human nature" - Plato

Bibliography

Abraham Lincoln's "failures" and "successes." (n.d.).
https://www.abrahamlincolnonline.org/lincoln/education/fail
ures.htm

Carnegie, D. (1981). *How to win friends and Influence People*. Simon &
Schuster.

Das, K. (2018). *Chants of a lifetime: Searching for a heart of gold*. Hay House,
Inc.

Famous quotes. Thomas Edison. (n.d.).
https://www.thomasedison.org/edison-quotes

Forbes Magazine. (2024, November 6). *Internet usage statistics in 2024*.
Forbes.

Hanna, J. (2017, August 14). Suicides under age 13: One every 5 days.
CNN.

Joyce, R., Sonja, Chase, Forbes, W. A., Dowling, G., Pl, & Garnier, T.
(2023, February 2). What's behind boom of Christianity in China?
Boston University.

Schleifstein, M. (2023, January 14). How many people died in
Hurricane Katrina? toll reduced 17 years later. NOLA.com.

Made in the USA
Las Vegas, NV
12 January 2025

16225071R00090